Berlin + Tokyo

Kosuke
Uchimura

jovis

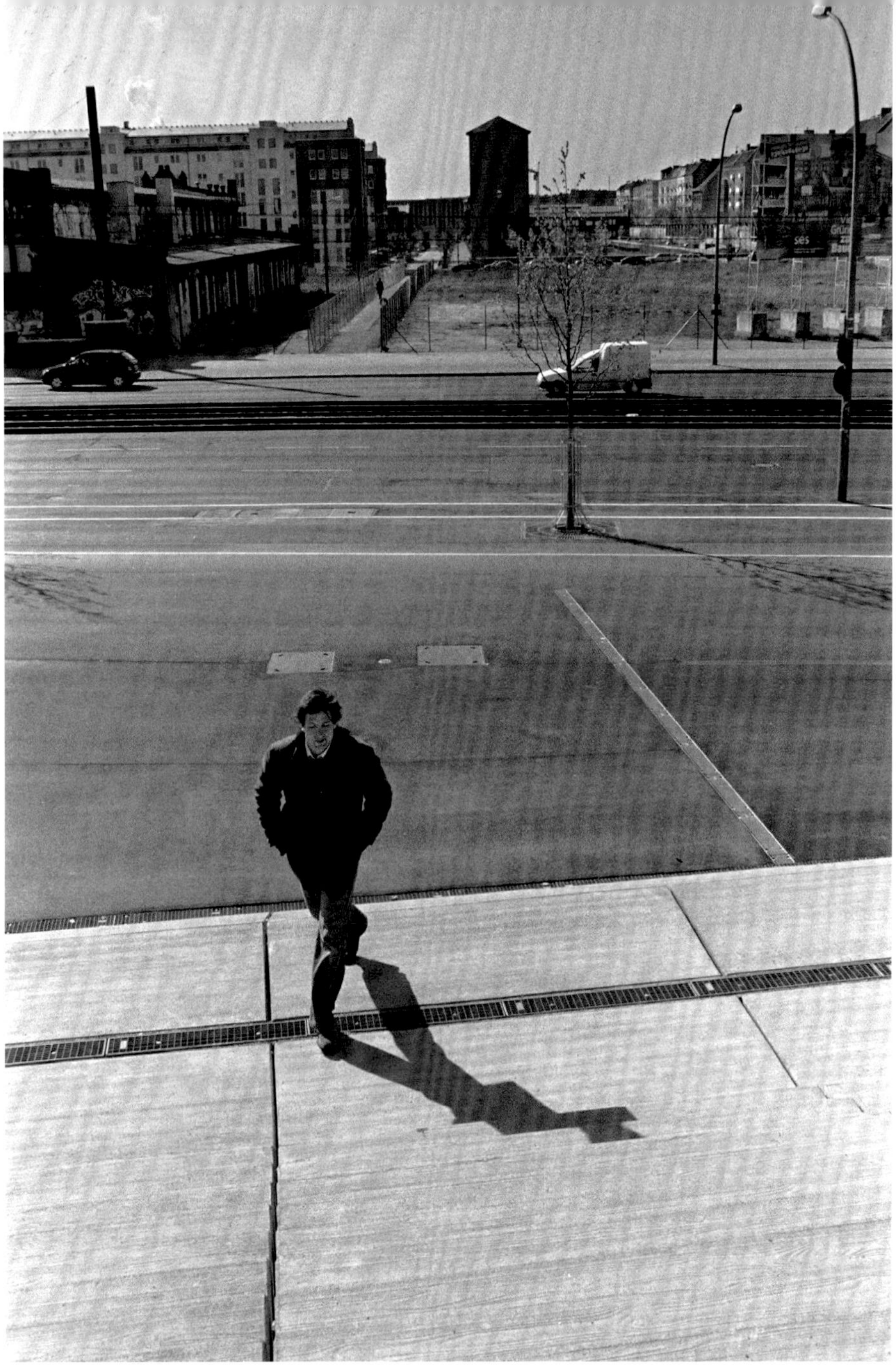

Berlin + Tokyo

Kosuke Uchimura

jovis

Besonderer Dank gebührt
Special thanks to

caco & Gosuke & Mame
Satoshi Matsumura, Takashi Yazaki
Chiaki Ikuta
Akihiko Yanagida, Yuko Nishimura, Yuki Mizoi
Misa Asai
Shizuka Kawahara
Ayuri Sakamoto

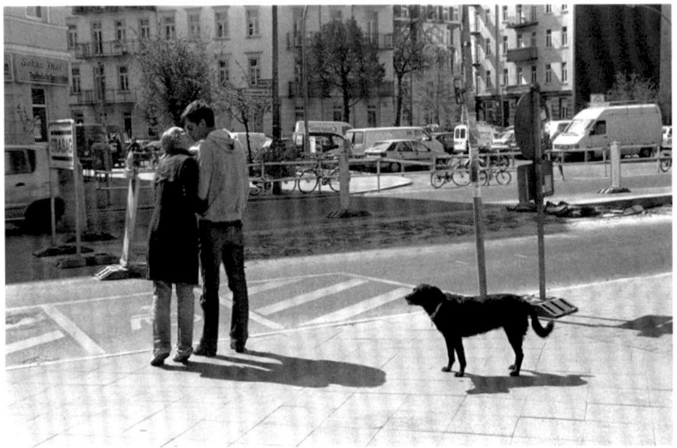

Impressum / Colophone

Übersetzung ins Deutsche / German translation: Shizuka Kawahara
Übersetzung ins Englische / English translation: Miwa Oishi
Englisches Lektorat / Copy-editing English: Inez Templeton
Gestaltung und Satz / Design and setting: Misa Asai
Titelgestaltung / Cover design: caco
Druck und Bindung / Printing and Binding:
OAN Offizin Andersen Nexö Leipzig, Zwenkau

Bibliografische Information Der Deutschen Bibliothek
Die Deutsche Bibliothek verzeichnet diese Publikation in der Deutschen Nationalbibliografie; detaillierte bibliografische Daten sind im Internet über http://dnb.ddb.de abrufbar.
Bibliographic information published by Die Deutsche Bibliothek
Die Deutsche Bibliothek lists this publication in the Deutsche Nationalbibliografie; detailed bibliographic data are available in the Internet at http://dnb.ddb.de

jovis Verlag
Kurfürstenstraße 15/16
10785 Berlin

www.jovis.de

ISBN: 978-3-939633-05-1

Berlin + Tokyo

Berlin und Tokyo – kaum jemand, am wenigsten Kenner beider Städte, würde spontan Gemeinsamkeiten zwischen diesen Metropolen vermuten. Und doch erscheinen sie mir wie Geschwister.

Betrachtet man nur das Stadtbild, ist davon zunächst nichts zu spüren. Während europäische Städte zumeist gründlich geplant und sorgfältig angelegt wurden, entwickelten sich asiatische Städte meist von selbst und wirken daher chaotisch, vor allem auf den westlichen Betrachter. Darüber hinaus widerspricht die europäische „Kultur des Steins", in der alte Gebäude immer wieder renoviert und instand gehalten werden, der asiatischen „Kultur des Holzes" mit ihren „Einweg"-Gebäuden.

„Immer wenn ich nach Berlin fahre, frage ich mich, was diese Stadt so einzigartig macht. Dabei suche ich nicht nach Gemeinsamkeiten mit Tokyo; vielmehr fallen mir im Vergleich die kulturellen Unterschiede auf." Dies sagt ein japanischer Wissenschaftler, der sich mit der deutschen Kultur beschäftigt und Deutschland regelmäßig besucht. Und sicher gilt sowohl für Fachleute als für Reisende, dass „Unterschiede" zwischen und somit auch die jeweiligen Einzigartigkeiten von Berlin und Tokyo umso deutlicher zutage treten, je besser man die beiden Metropolen und ihre jeweilige Kultur kennt.

Ich selbst bin weder Experte für Urbanistik noch für Architektur. Ich bin Fotograf, und seit langem schon ist Tokyo mein bevorzugtes Motiv. Es sind die Menschen auf den Straßen dieser Stadt, bemerkenswerte Szenen und Gegenstände, ja sogar Geräusche, die ich mit meiner Kamera festzuhalten versucht habe, während ich mich durch die Stadt treiben ließ. Aus dem Moment heraus entstanden, zeigen meine Aufnahmen von Tokyo meist zufällige und einmalige Anblicke.

Man kann sich fragen, warum ich mein Leben dieser Tätigkeit gewidmet habe, die weder Reichtum noch besonderen Ruhm verspricht? Wegen der einflussreichen Werke von Henri Cartier-Bresson und Ihei Kimur, die mich als Schüler zur Fotografie brachten? Das ist sicher ein Grund. Oder war ich auf der Suche nach meiner Identität als Japaner? Schließlich bin ich in Burma geboren und habe zwei Drittel meiner Jugendzeit in Kanada und Großbritannien verbracht. Sicherlich ist auch deswegen Tokyo mein bevorzugtes Motiv geworden.

Dies heißt aber nicht, dass ich mich mit der Stadt so sehr identifiziere, dass die Fotografien, die ich von ihr mache, eigentlich Abbilder meiner selbst sind – in der Tat spiegeln die Großstadtbilder vieler erfolgreicher Fotografen meiner Generation immer zuallererst die Persönlichkeit des Fotografen wider.

Meine Fotografien sind in diesem Sinne unvollständig. Natürlich bildet jede Aufnahme, selbst wenn der Auslöser versehentlich gedrückt wird, in gewisser Weise den Menschen ab, der sie macht. Und insofern kann ich nicht leugnen, dass sich auch mein „Selbst" irgendwo in meinen Bildern wiederfindet. Doch ich versuche stets, den jeweiligen Gegenstand meiner Aufnahmen selbst zum Sprechen zu bringen, ihn zum „Subjekt" des Bildes zu machen, anstatt ihn durch meine subjektive Interpretation zu überlagern. Was die Menschen und Dinge auf meinen Bildern ausdrücken, war mir immer wichtiger als der

Ausdruck meiner eigenen Persönlichkeit. Ich sehe mit den Augen eines „Zuschauers" auf die Stadt. Und das ist der Grund, warum ich Tokyo fotografiere: nichts anderes als der Wunsch, die faszinierende Atmosphäre dieser Stadt einzufangen. Ich will die Stadt mit der Kamera erspüren.

Gewiss: In Tokyo herrscht Tag und Nacht ungeheurer Lärm, die Bevölkerungsdichte ist entsetzlich, die Oberflächlichkeit der Menschen ist abstoßend, im Sommer werden Hitze und Luftfeuchtigkeit unerträglich. Und doch: Diese Stadt ist auf ihre ganz eigene Art unwiderstehlich. Ihre Straßen und Gebäude, das flirrende Leben, das hier unaufhörlich pulsiert – das zu erleben, versöhnt einen immer wieder mit Tokyo.

Aber was genau ist es, das Tokyo so besonders macht? Lassen Sie mich zuerst von Berlin und Deutschland erzählen. Im Jahr 1984, als ich noch in London lebte, habe ich zum ersten Mal Berlin besucht – damals teilte die Mauer noch die Stadt. Mein Vater, ein Diplomat, brachte uns mit dem Auto von der Ostseite an die vorderste Front

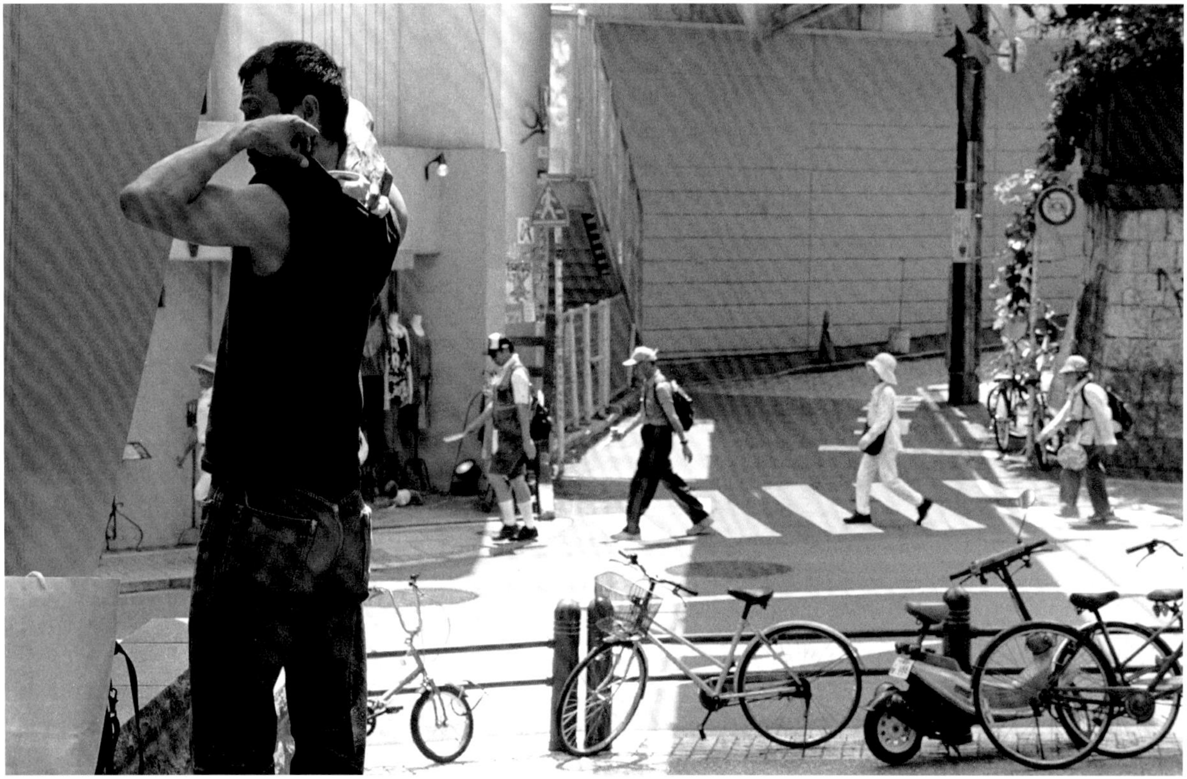

des Kalten Krieges. Ich war noch ein Kind und es fällt mir schwer, in Worte zu fassen, was ich damals empfand. Auf jeden Fall war ich tief beeindruckt. Nicht von der „Schönheit" oder „Erhabenheit" der Stadt – Worte wie diese wären zur Beschreibung des damaligen Berlin sicherlich vollkommen fehl am Platze. Aber ich fühlte mich dieser auf abnorme Weise zerrissenen Stadt, die so ganz anders war als London oder Paris, auf seltsame Weise verbunden.

Seit ich 12 oder 13 war, hat mich das „Deutsche" fasziniert. Wie alle anderen Jungen in diesem Alter liebte ich es, mit Panzern und Kampfflugzeugen zu spielen, und am meisten mochte ich die deutschen (die deutschen Waffen, Flug- und Fahrzeuge aus dem Zweiten Weltkrieg sind in Deutschland zwar ein Tabu, aber in Japan sind sie als Spielzeug sehr beliebt bei den Kindern). Mit meinen Freunden wetteiferte ich darum, wer das schönste Modell eines Tiger-Panzers anfertigen konnte. Ich begann, mich für die deutsche Zeitgeschichte und die Kultur des Landes zu interessieren. Nachdem ich während der Fußballweltmeisterschaft 1982 Karl-Heinz Rummenigge und Pierre Littbarski erlebt hatte, begann ich selbst Fußball zu spielen. Als ich in London wohnte, entdeckte ich die klassische Musik, und besonders Mozart (zwar Österreicher) faszinierte mich. Eine Oper des zeitgenössischen Komponisten Karlheinz Stockhausen, die ich im Covent Garden sah, war für mich wie ein Schock und hatte großen Einfluss auf mein Empfindungsvermögen. Zurück in Japan, zu Beginn meiner Laufbahn als Fotograf, verehrte ich die Filme von Wim Wenders. Zurzeit fahre ich einen Volkswagen und fotografiere mit Carl-Zeiss-Objektiven. Dabei war all dies nicht das Ergebnis einer gezielten Suche, sondern hat sich eher zufällig, wie von selbst ergeben.

Meine Faszination für Berlin beruht, neben meiner persönlichen „Germanophilie", sicherlich auf den eindrucksvollen Bildern des ersten Besuches. In gewisser Weise hängt sie aber auch mit meiner Liebe zu Tokyo zusammen. Und als mir bei meinem zweiten Berlinbesuch im Frühjahr 2005 plötzlich klar wurde, wie sehr sich die beiden Städte ähneln, hatte ich die Idee zu diesem Buch. Eigentlich wollte ich mir damals, auf Empfehlung eines befreundeten Architekten, die neue Architektur der wiedervereinigten Stadt ansehen, den intensiven Um- und Aufbau Berlins. Die Fotos, die ich während dieses Besuchs machte, berührten mich jedoch auf ganz unerwartete Weise: Keines der vielen Bilder, die ich bis dahin von den Straßen von London, Kopenhagen, Kalkutta, Taipei, Hongkong, Bangkok oder Chengdu (China) gemacht hatte, hatte irgendeine Verbindung zu meinem großen Tokyo-Projekt gehabt. Sie sprachen eine fremde Sprache. In Berlin ist das anders – wenn ich hier fotografiere, fühle ich dasselbe wie in Tokyo. Auch wenn ich weiß, dass ich im Ausland bin, verstehe ich die Botschaft der Stadt, als wäre es meine eigene.

Welche Botschaft das ist? Das kann ich mit Worten nicht sagen. Ich kann nur versuchen, es mittels meiner Fotografien auszudrücken. Sehen Sie sich die Bilder an!

Hier nur einige Aspekte zur Ergänzung: Berlin wie Tokyo erstanden neu aus den Trümmern des Zweiten Weltkriegs. Dabei wurde Berlin, besonders West-Berlin, zum großen Teil tatsächlich wiederaufgebaut, der alte Stadtgrundriss und das architektonische Erscheinungsbild wurden weitgehend beibehalten. In Tokyo hingegen ließ man zwar den Stadtgrundriss unangetastet, aber das Bild des modernen Tokyo hat keinerlei Ähnlichkeit mehr mit der Vorkriegsstadt.

Mit der deutschen Wiedervereinigung kam in Berlin erneut ein Umbauprozess in Gang, der noch längst nicht abgeschlossen ist. Und Tokyo ist schon seit Kriegsende in unaufhörlicher Veränderung begriffen. In beiden Städten ist deshalb eine Dynamik zu spüren, die „vollendeten" Städten wie zum Beispiel Prag oder Kyoto, Japans alter Hauptstadt, völlig abgeht. Der krasse Kontrast von Alt und Neu, wie er einem in Tokyo auf Schritt und Tritt begegnet, findet sich in Europa in dieser Form eigentlich nur in Berlin.

Die japanische wie die deutsche Hauptstadt haben beide mehrere Zentren mit ganz unterschiedlichem Charakter: in Berlin zum Beispiel der Kurfürstendamm im ehemaligen West-Berlin und der Alexanderplatz und Mitte im ehemaligen Ost-Berlin. Tokyo hat Asakusa und Ueno, die Vergnügungsviertel der Vorkriegszeit, Shinjuku und Shibuya, die Vergnügungsviertel der Nachkriegszeit; dazwischen liegt Ginza, das alte Handelsviertel. Außerdem wird in beiden Städten die Innenstadt von einem Stadtbahnring umschlossen, in Berlin von der S-Bahn, in Tokyo von der JR Line, was in anderen Großstädten selten der Fall ist.

Die Teilung der Stadt hat Berlin tief geprägt. Bis heute findet man große Unterschiede zwischen den östlichen und westlichen Stadtteilen und ihren Bewohnern. Doch auch Tokyo ist geteilt: in das tiefer gelegene Shitamachi („Unterstadt") im Osten und das höher gelegene, hügelige Yamanote („Oberstadt") im Westen. Shitamachi war schon

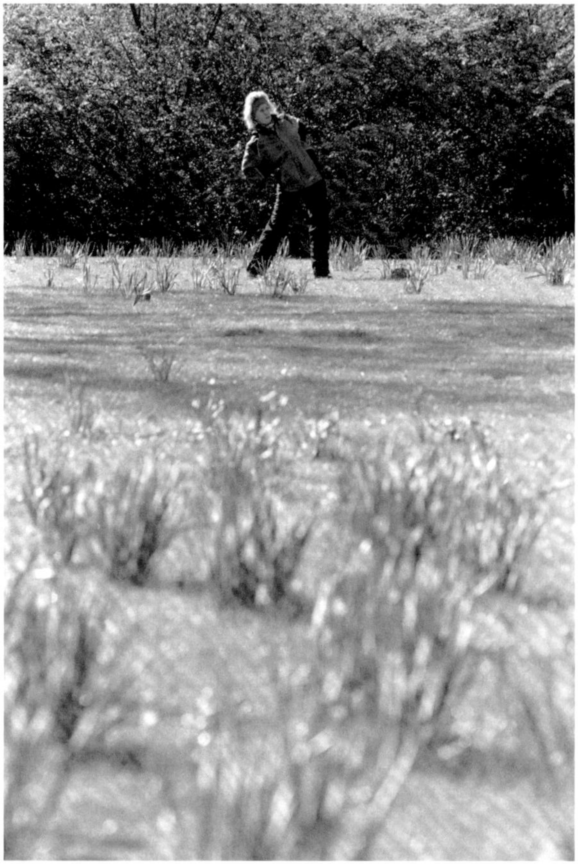

immer der volkstümlichere Stadtteil, traditionell der Wohnort der einfachen Leute. Im eleganten Yamanote dagegen leben die Zugezogenen. Aber die charakteristischen alten Geschäfte und Häuser von Shitamachi beginnen nach und nach zu verschwinden, und viele sagen, dass der Unterschied zwischen Shitamachi und Yamanote nur noch in den Namen erkennbar wäre. Ich halte das aber für falsch, ganz im Gegenteil: Der Unterschied wird deutlicher. Ich kann das nicht mit soziologischen Daten belegen oder anhand von ökonomischen und politischen Veränderungen in Japan erklären, aber ich fotografiere die Stadt und ihre Bewohner seit Jahren und kann die Unterschiede deutlich sehen und benennen: auf der einen Seite das gemächliche, gesetzte Shitamachi, auf der anderen Seite das geschäftige, hektische Yamanote – in gewisser Weise gleichen Sie dem West- und dem Ostteil Berlins.

Sicherlich ließen sich weitere Gemeinsamkeiten aufführen, zum Beispiel, dass Japaner wie Deutsche als fleißig, ordnungsliebend und formell gelten – aber ich möchte das nicht weiter ausführen. Zur Erklärung meiner Bilder mögen die bisherigen Betrachtungen ausreichen. Schließlich zielt kein einziges Bild vordergründig auf eines der angesprochenen Themen ab. Alle Motive sind nichts weiter als zufällig gewählte Ausschnitte aus einem beziehungsreichen Gesamtbild.

Jedenfalls habe ich – als Weiterführung meines Tokyoter Langzeitprojekts – im Frühling 2005 und im Winter 2006 Berlin erneut besucht und fotografiert. Danach habe ich die Fotos von Berlin und Tokyo wie Spielkarten gemischt, und wie erwartet haben die Bilder nahezu von selbst eine neue Welt ergeben. Ich habe Bilder ausgewählt, auf denen die besondere Beziehung zwischen Berlin und Tokyo deutlich wird, und sie einander gegenüber gestellt – so entstand dieses Buch. Weil es aber langweilig wäre, Bilder, die die gleichen Situationen zeigen, miteinander zu konfrontieren, habe ich ein subtileres Auswahlprinzip gewählt. Die Doppelseiten des Buches zeigen Eindrücke, die sich trotz aller Unterschiede in gewisser Weise ähneln, aber auch unterscheiden, trotz aller Gemeinsamkeiten. Damit verknüpft ist die geheime Hoffnung, die das + in „Berlin + Tokyo" ausdrückt – dass aus ihnen ein neues Stadtbild entsteht, das weder Berlin noch Tokyo ist.

Shitamachi, Tokyo

Kosuke Uchimura

Berlin + Tokyo

"Berlin and Tokyo are alike" … or so I am convinced prior to publicizing my photographs. Yet there will be hardly anyone who would concur with such a remark; least of all of those who have been to and seen both cities. Generally speaking, the "orderliness" of European cities, which is based on thorough town planning, contrasts the naturally derived state of "disorderliness" found in Asian cities. There is also a fundamental difference between a "stone culture" in which a single built architecture is maintained and used throughout the ages; and that of "wood culture" which is prone to consumption. These features are evident in cities representing Europe and Asia such as Berlin and Tokyo, and the two cities are in fact heterogeneous as urban spheres.

"Whenever I visit Berlin, I end up wondering what the attraction of this city is. Rather than experiencing something in common between Berlin and Tokyo, I tend to compare the two and experience the differences existing between each urban culture." This is a comment made by a Japanese scholar, who researches German culture and makes frequent visits to Germany. Those whose knowledge of cities and cultures is more cultivated, tend to have a more accurate grasp of the "difference" between Germany (Berlin) and Japan (Tokyo), and are able to discern the unique characteristics of each city. I think this is the right perspective for both specialists and travellers.

I am neither a specialist in urban theory nor in architectural studies; I am a photographer, and have long been in contact with the city called Tokyo. As a matter of fact, I have been shooting passers-by coming and going in the streets of Tokyo; multifarious strange objects found along the streets; and the ambience created by the bustle and confusion of differing seasons – all through the mechanical eye of a so-called camera. I am not interested in particular people living in Tokyo or in particular streets. Always with a camera in my hand, I just stroll through the streets of the city and take pictures of scenes as I encounter them – particular moments and occasions that will never recur in one's lifetime.

What has driven me to commit such acts, which will certainly never lead to fame, as my part of daily life? Is it because of the works of Henri Cartier-Bresson and Ihei Kimura, which inspired me during my teens when I first began photography? That is true in part. Alternatively, has being born in Burma and spending two-thirds of my youth in Canada and Britain driven me to recover and compensate for my lack of Japanese identity by keeping my eyes fixed upon Tokyo? I believe this is closer to truth than the Bresson and Kimura story.

Still, had I truly wanted to overlap my own identity with Tokyo, I would be embedding my flesh and spirit more into a city called Tokyo, and would have fixed my own "self" amidst the images I take. In reality, most of my peer photographers are achieving success by taking snaps of Tokyo or other "cities in which one relates oneself more deeply" or "landscape that projects oneself."

In that regard, my photographs are half measures. As long as he who presses the shutter is a human self possessed with sensibility, that very "self" comes out in the photograph

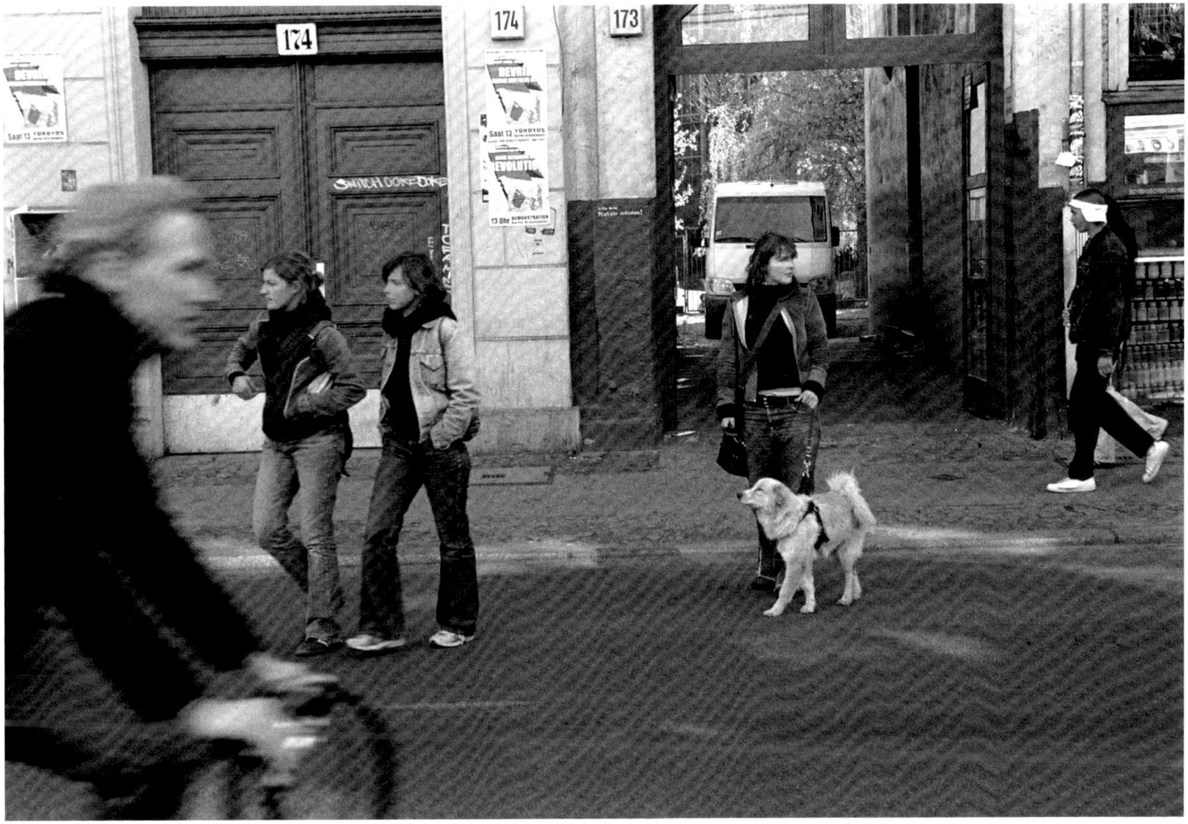

even though he has pressed it unwillingly. In that sense, I will not deny that my own "self" is inevitably reflected in my photographs, too. Nevertheless, it is also true that I have a strong urge to bring out, as much as possible, a certain message carried by the subject in a photograph (rather than imposing my own subjective interpretation on the subject.) In terms of balancing between "my own subjective sensibility" and "the message delivered by the subject itself," I have been photographing Tokyo by giving more weight to the latter. Hence, without becoming too involved in Tokyo, I come to see things more as a bystander when I am holding my camera.

At one time, I used to question my own conscience as a photographer, but now I have no such delusions. This is because I simply find comfort in exposing myself to an air that Tokyo emits, which is the greatest reason why I continue to photograph this city. By drawing out such sensations with my camera, I have come to realize that I want to feel this city to the fullest. Undoubtedly, Tokyo is surrounded by much noise and by people driven by their vanities. Moreover, the population density is sickeningly high and both the temperature and humidity levels are too high during the summer. Setting aside such abominable aspects, the particular feel of that air that forms the basis of the city – and by that I mean the whole air emitted by the people and objects in the streets together with the expressions of various streetscapes – are all somehow pleasing.

Before going on to reveal the real identity of that particular pleasantness of Tokyo, I would like to talk about Berlin and Germany. The first time I visited Berlin was in 1984 when I used to live in London. I entered the divided city from the east side of the Cold War frontline, in a car driven by my father who used to be a diplomat. I had not yet started photography at the time, and since we were just touring around on a family excursion, it would be difficult to express in exact words what I felt then, but the experience definitely left a powerful impression on me. Words of praise such as "beautiful" or "sublime" would not apply; however, I felt a strange sympathy towards an air that was obviously different from that in London or Paris. Also, taking into account the abnormal condition of the East-West divide, the whole city emitted such a peculiar air.

To begin with, I have favoured "things that are Germanic" since my childhood. I must have been twelve or thirteen when they fascinated me for the first time. Like many boys in my age group, I used to love tanks and battle planes. My particular favourites were German made (German weapons of WWII now regarded as a kind of taboo in Germany are among the most popular plastic models sold in Japan.). I used to compete with my friends in building the plastic model of a Tiger tank. From that time, I slowly started to develop an interest in modern history and the culture of Germany. I began to play football out of admiration for the performances of Rummenigge and Littbarski, who played active parts in the World Cup at the time. During my London years, I also became interested in classical music, and was particularly devoted to Mozart (though he was an Austrian). I liked contemporary music too, and was particularly struck by a new production of an opera by Stockhausen at the Royal Opera House in Covent Garden, which was to have a great influence on my sensibilities. After returning to Japan, I started photography and was devoted to Wim Wenders' cinematography. Now, I go out in my Volkswagen and take photographs with Carl Zeiss lenses. These are not consciously acquired tastes; it would be more accurate to say, "I have somehow come to acquire them over the course of time".

What lies at the root of my fascination for Berlin is no doubt both the striking image I received upon my first visit during the period of the city's division, and my personal "Germanophile" sensibility. Yet, it is true that this is also linked to my "Tokyophile" sensibility, which I mentioned earlier on. This is because an electrifying intuition that "Berlin and Tokyo are alike," felt upon my second visit to Berlin in the winter of 2005, inspired me to publicize this photographic collection.

The original purpose of my second visit to Berlin was to take a look at the city's modern architecture. As a streetscape photographer, I was already interested in architecture. Another reason I visited Berlin was because an architect friend of mine told me that, "following re-unification, the modern architecture in Berlin, which is going through extensive redevelopment, is really worth seeing." Eventually, I visited Berlin with my architect friend and another old friend who is in interior design. Beyond the insights gained from the architecture itself, the street photos I took during my architectural tours clicked more with my sensibilities than I expected.

Up until then, I had taken street photos in different foreign cities such as London, Copenhagen, Calcutta (India), Taipei, Hong Kong, Bangkok, and Chengdu (China). Even so, they were taken just for those occasions and never really linked to my lifework streetscapes of Tokyo. After all, the implications of those images taken abroad as well as the air emitted were of foreign nature to me. Yet in Berlin, I can take photographs with exactly the same feel as I do back in Tokyo. When taking photographs in Berlin, though the view that stretches before me is foreign, my mood is the same as when I am in Tokyo. In other words: in Berlin I can get the same message out of the city as I have already received elsewhere in Tokyo with the same sensibilities.

If I were asked what, then, are the same kind of messages, I would actually be stuck for an accurate answer. To be honest, I am unable to express these messages in words, so I express them through my photographs: just take a look at them before anything…! That would, however, be slightly rash guidance, so let me explore the objective aspects of my own expression.

If I were to raise certain commonalities between today's Berlin and Tokyo, first I would say that both cities were rebuilt from the ashes and ruins of the Second World War. Berlin, and in particular, West Berlin, was rebuilt by retaining its original city layout and architectural traces. In the case of Tokyo, although the original city layout remained fundamentally unchanged, it is different from Berlin in that its new buildings are completely different in both form and style from those of the pre-war era. Nevertheless, Berlin, which is still under construction after the fall of the Berlin Wall, and Tokyo, which continues to change ceaselessly after the war, both embrace a growing energy of motion that is undetectable in almost perfected cities such as Prague or the ancient capital of Japan, Kyoto. Tokyo, where both old and new architectures exist in drastic clutters as a matter of course is a rare cityscape in Europe, except perhaps in Berlin, where it also attracts attention.

The second common factor lies in the patterns of both cities. They are arranged so that they both form several central areas. In Berlin, the Kurfürstendamm environs of former West Berlin and Alexanderplatz environs as well as Mitte of former East Berlin, form the central parts. Similarly, in Tokyo, there are the pre-war red-light districts of Asakusa and Ueno, and Shinjuku and Shibuya that thrived as the post-war red-light districts, and in between lies Ginza, which has been the central commercial district since the pre-war era. Both Berlin and Tokyo are similar in that both cities have several central areas with separate roles and individual characters within them. Furthermore, both cities have similar rail systems encircling their central areas (S-Bahn in Berlin and JR lines in Tokyo), which are not so common in other big cities.

The East-West divide is a fact peculiar to Berlin, and even now, the streets and atmosphere of people seem entirely different between the two parts of the city. This actually applies to Tokyo too. Tokyo is divided greatly into a geographically low-lying eastern part known as "Shitamachi" (literally meaning "lower town", or districts lower than Edo castle) and the western part of the hilly residential quarter known as "Yamanote" (literally meaning "upper town"). Generally speaking, "Shitamachi" is known as the traditional town of shopping and entertainment for commoners since the old times, and "Yamanote" is known as the sophisticated quarter where people from the whole of Japan are gathered. In recent times, those old and characteristic rows of traditional stores and houses in "Shitamachi" are beginning to fade away. Hence it is said that the traditional distinction between "Shitamachi" and "Yamanote" tends to exist only in their names. I, however, would not agree. Rather, the distinction is becoming increasingly visible to me. Since I am not a sociologist, I am not qualified to explain my reasons by referring to economic and political changes in Japan. Still, as one who has been taking photographs of Tokyo over many years, I can testify that I can clearly see and tell the difference in the occupants and the atmosphere between the two areas. Modest and composed "Shitamachi" and dazzling and hectic "Yamanote" bear a similar contrast to that between former East and West Berlin.

Certainly, there are other commonalities that are generally spoken of, such as both nations sharing similar national characteristics of being hard working and formal, but let me end here. Actually, as far as I wish to talk about my photographic collections, there wouldn't be much point in continuing my musings, since there is not a single photograph that directly reflects the issues or themes that I have mentioned so far. To the best of my ability, my photographs of individual taste are no more than clippings of an evocative air, probably common to and reflective of such issues and themes.

Be that as it may, as an extended lifework activity of Tokyo, I visited Berlin and took photographs in the spring

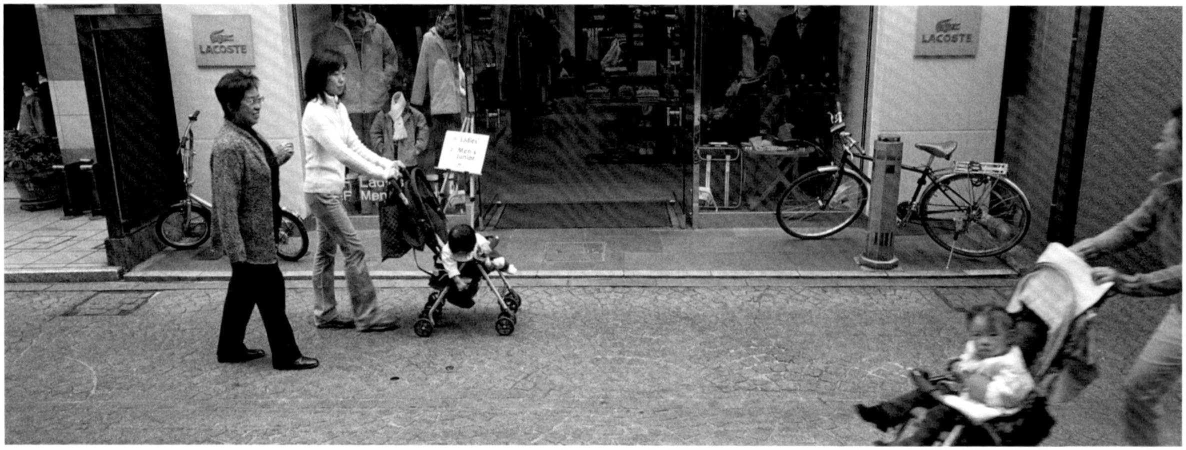

of 2005 and the winter of the following year. Then I shuffled the completed photographs of Berlin and Tokyo like a pack of cards. As I expected, they intermingled without any unfamiliarity and formed a world of their own. Out of such photographs, I have selected those that display the likeness between Berlin and Tokyo in juxtapositions, which are displayed in this photographic collection of "Berlin + Tokyo."

However, I found it to be rather boring to merely juxtapose photographs of Berlin and Tokyo that obviously display the same situations. Consequently, I have tried as much as possible to select those photographs that are subtly linked to each other. They are the ones which "seem different yet are somehow alike," or "are alike yet somehow different." Yet they are not just "alike" or "different" in categories. They derive a secret hope from the "+" bit of "Berlin + Tokyo" – that they will give birth to a new urban sphere which belongs to neither categories.

Shitamachi, Tokyo

Kosuke Uchimura

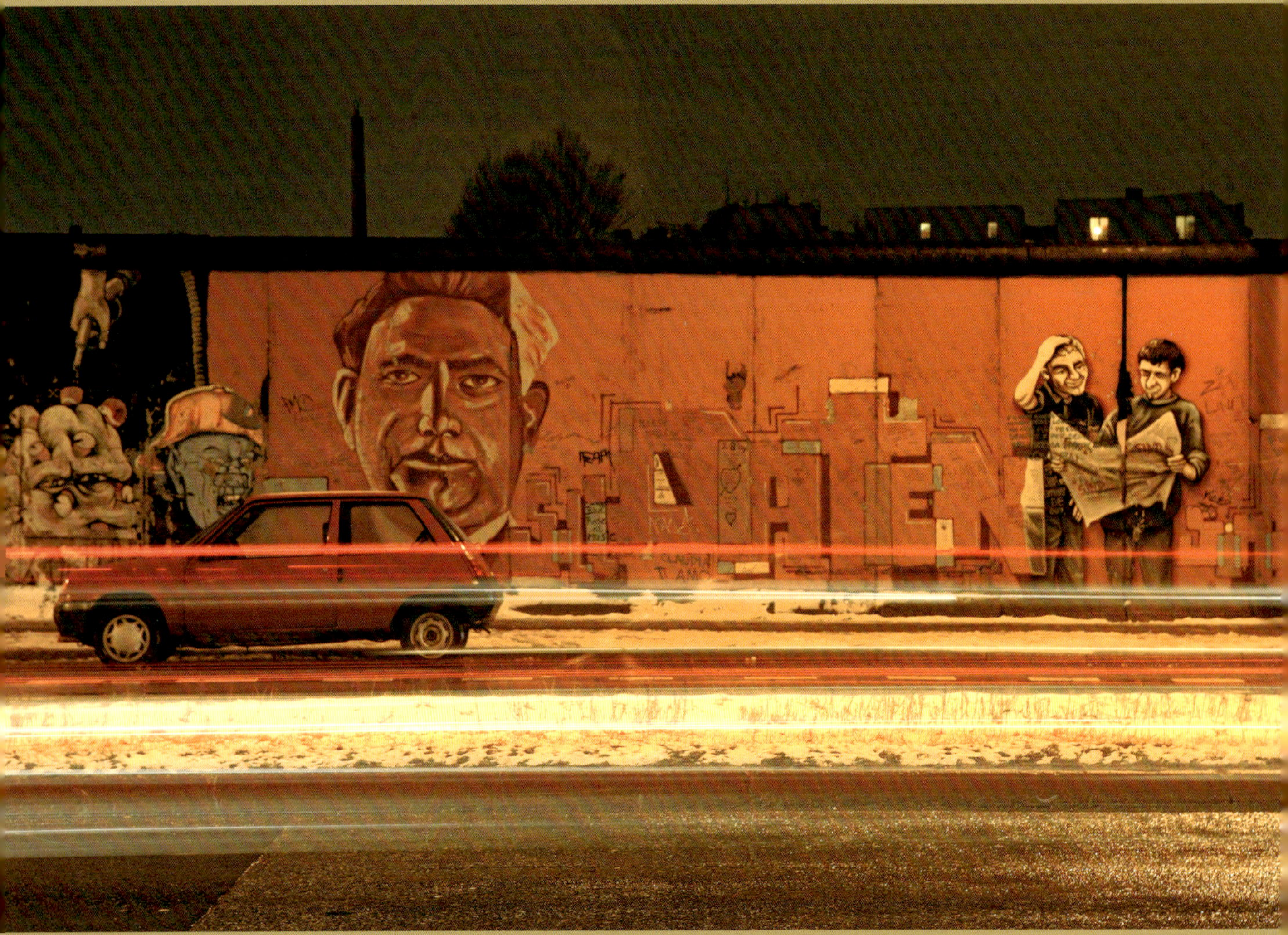

East Side Galle

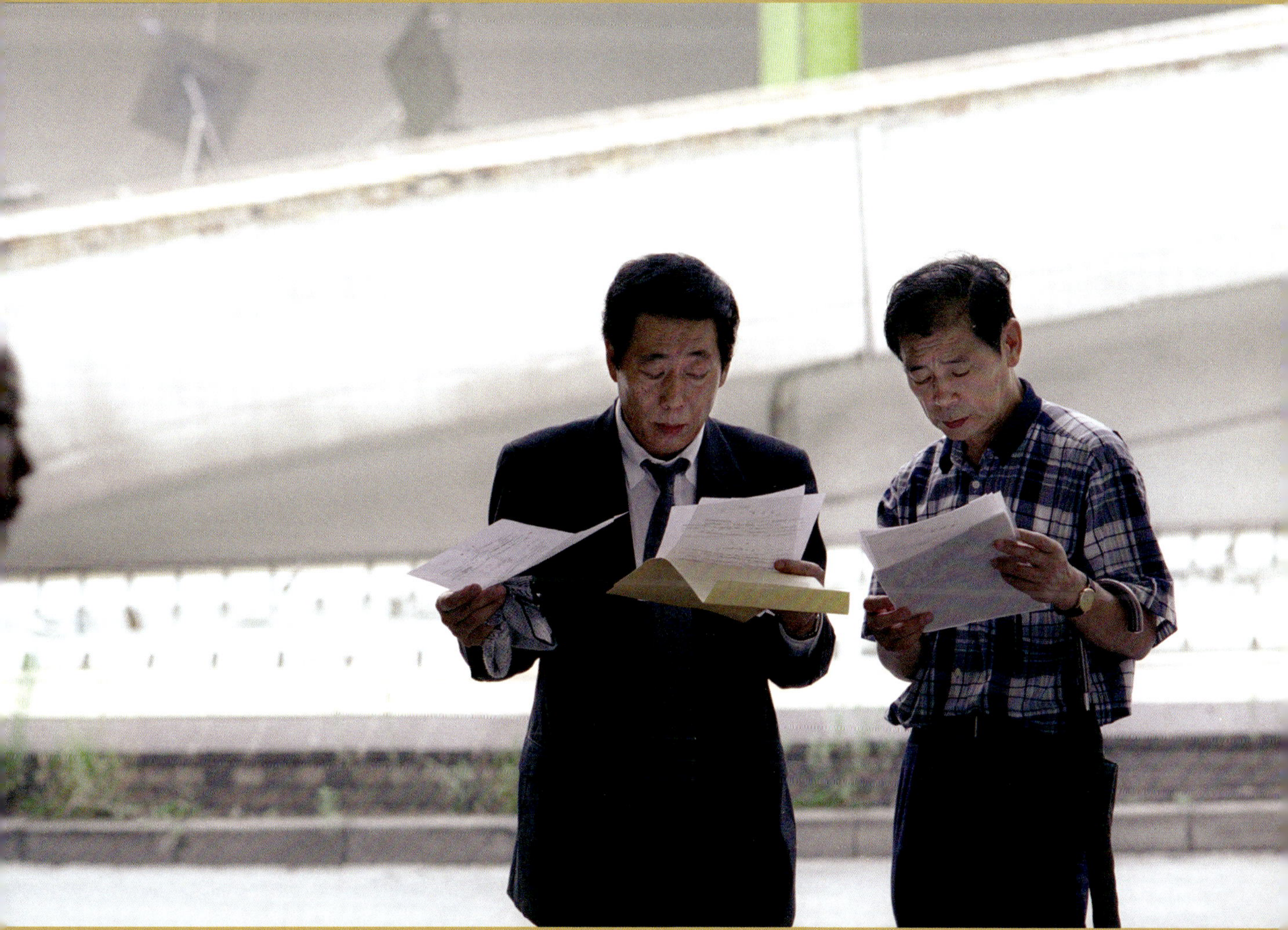

Shinjyuku

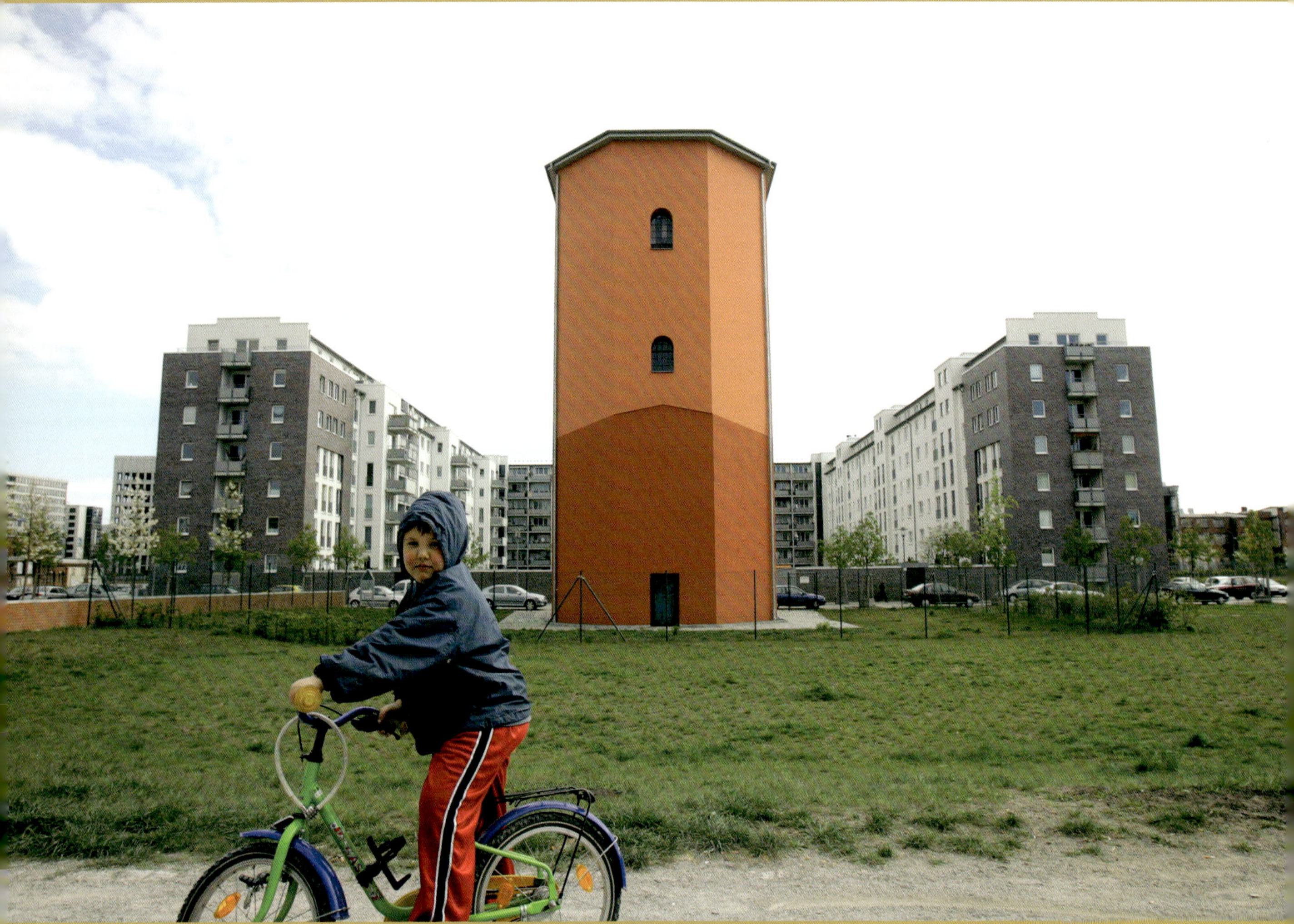

Prenzlauer Be

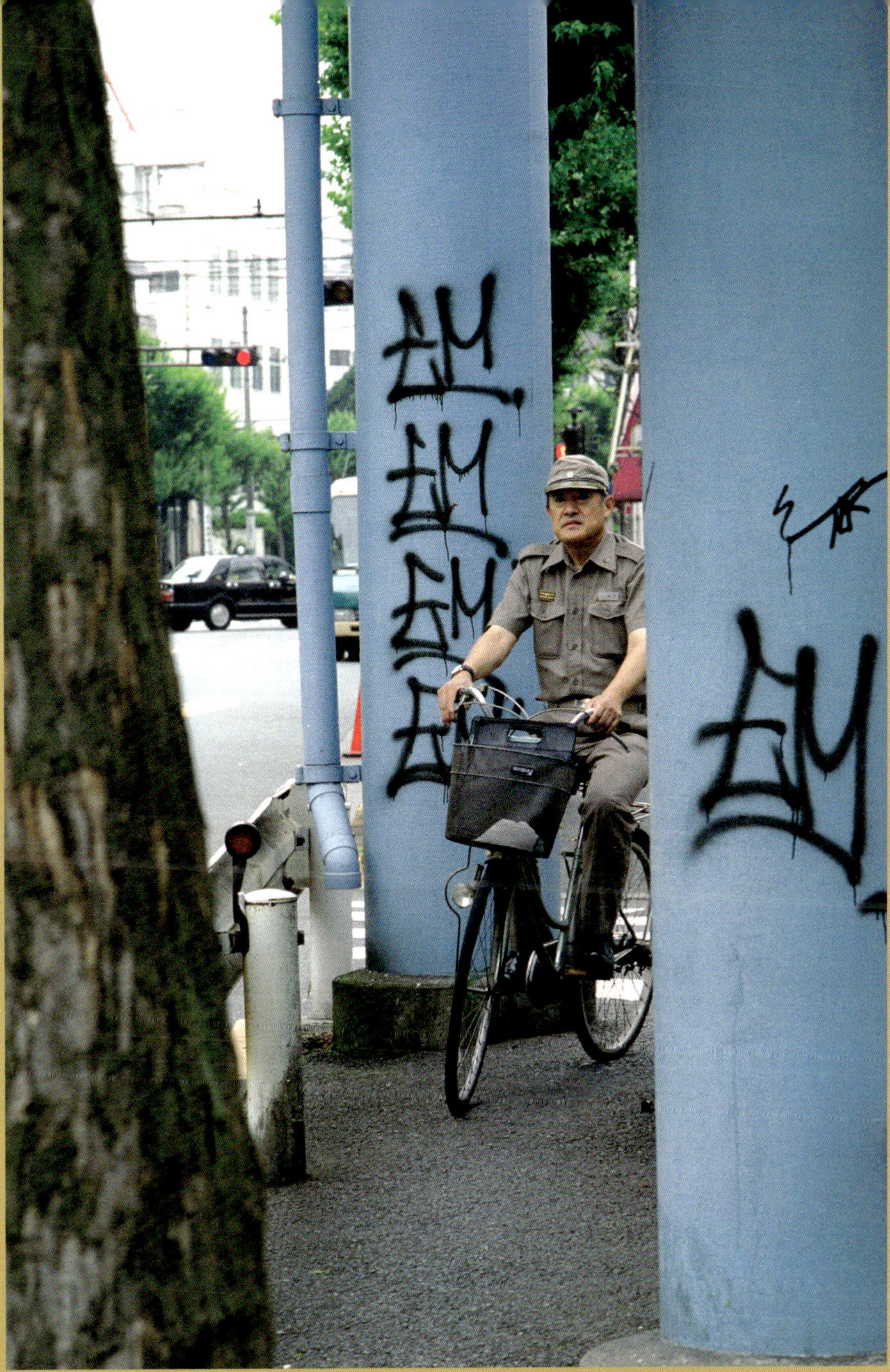

Musashikoyama

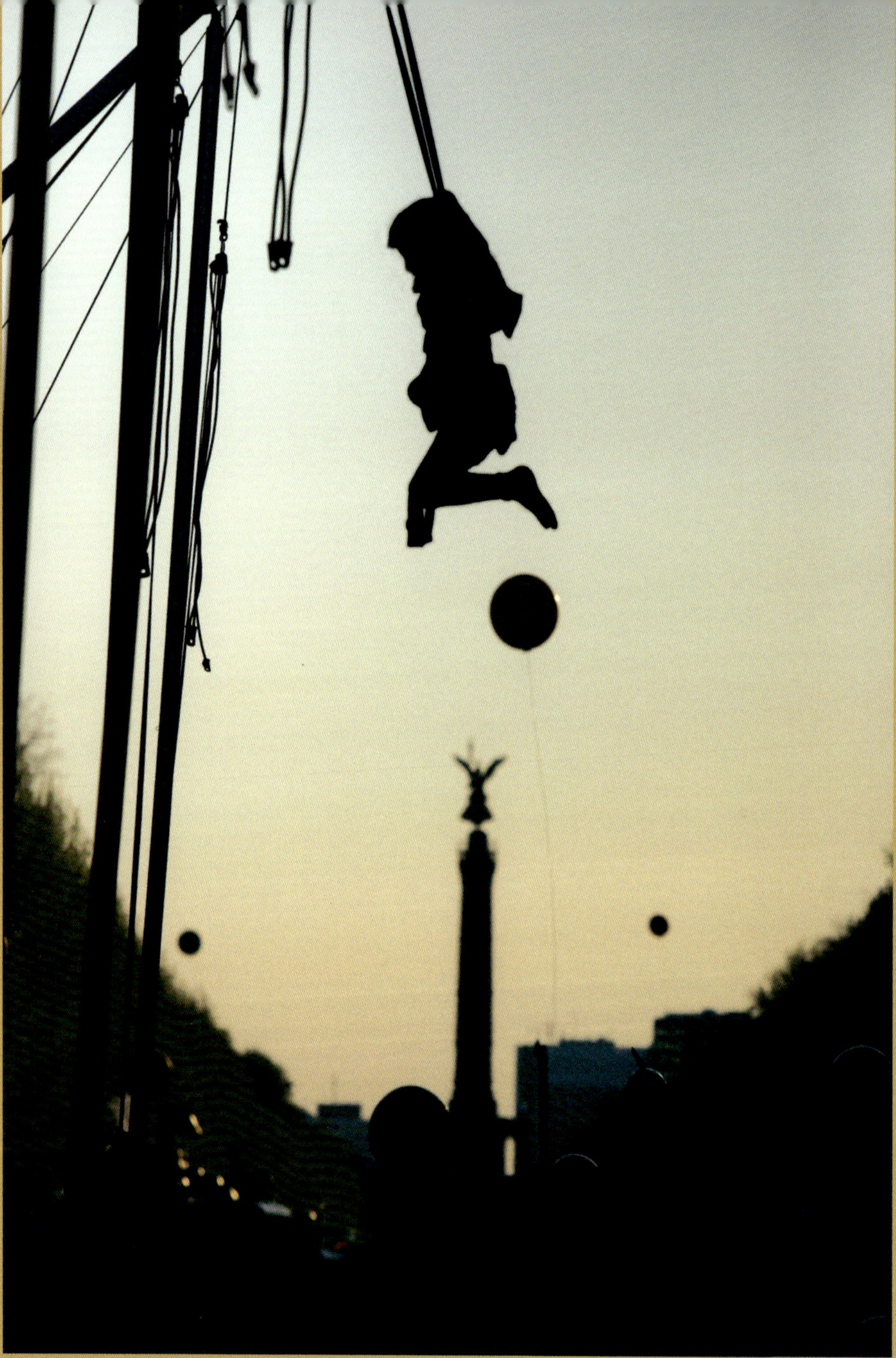

Straße des 17. Juni

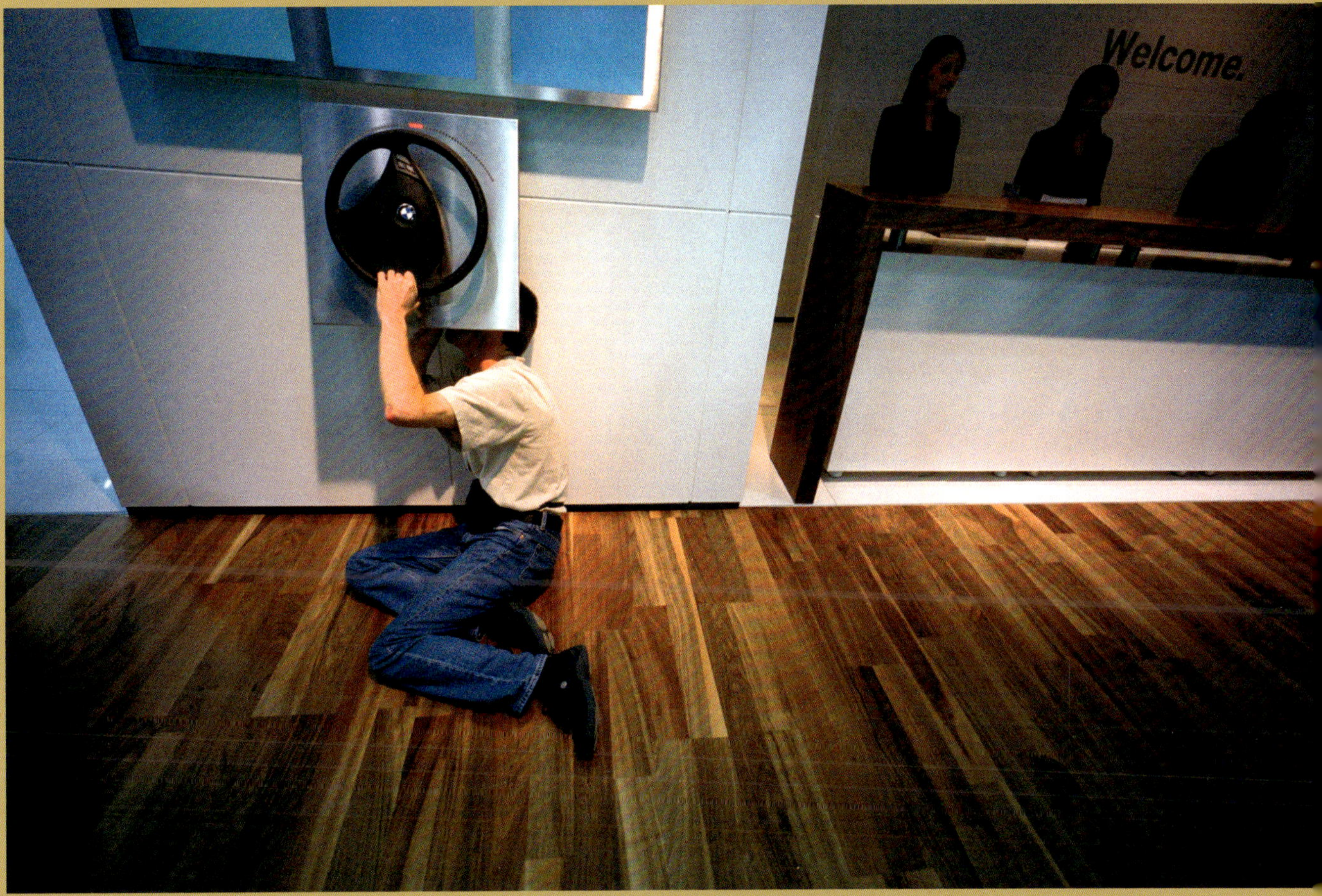

Tokyo Motor Show

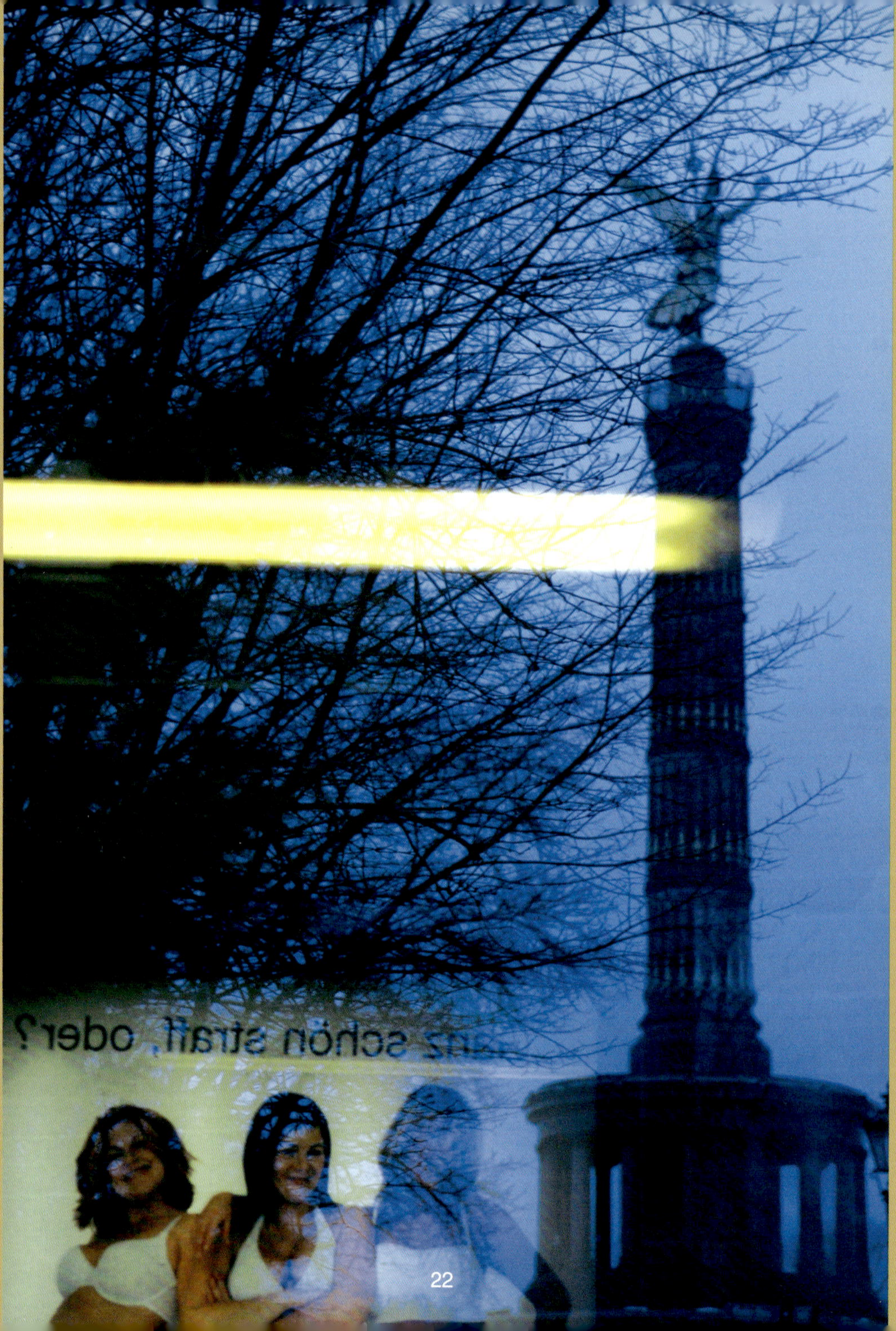

Siegessäule

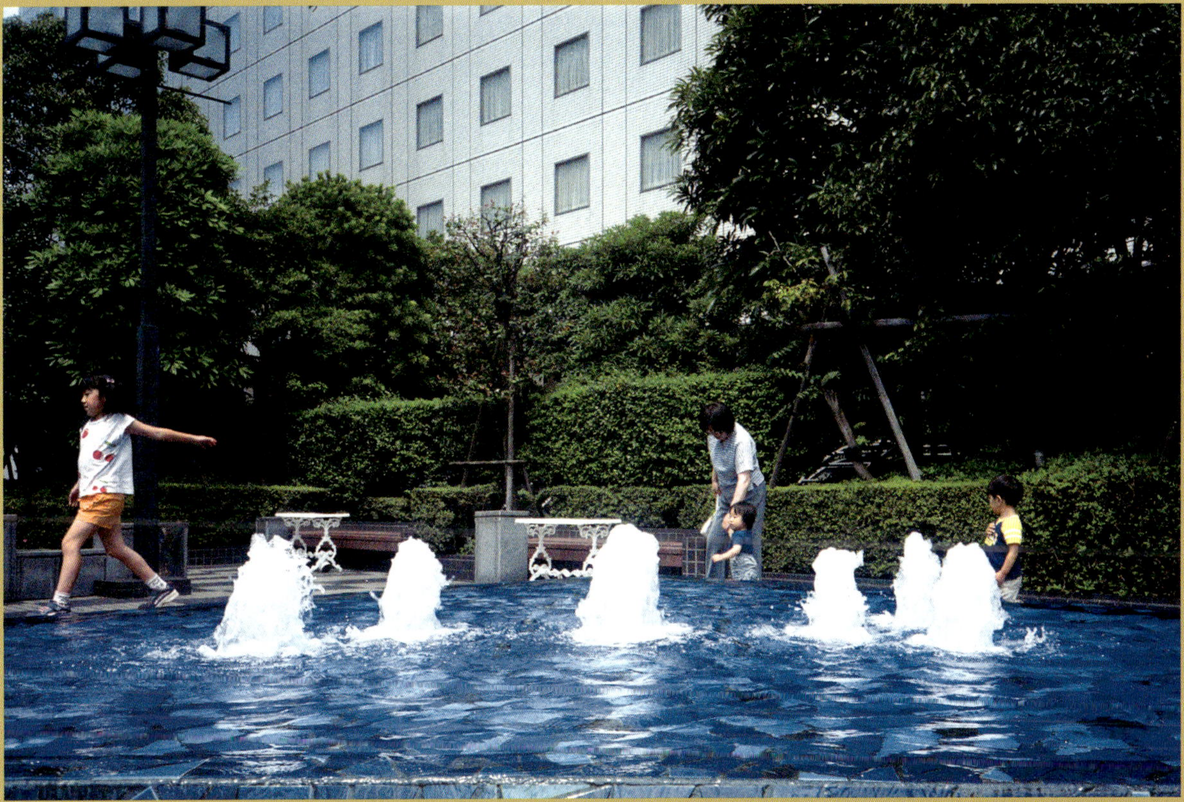

Osaki

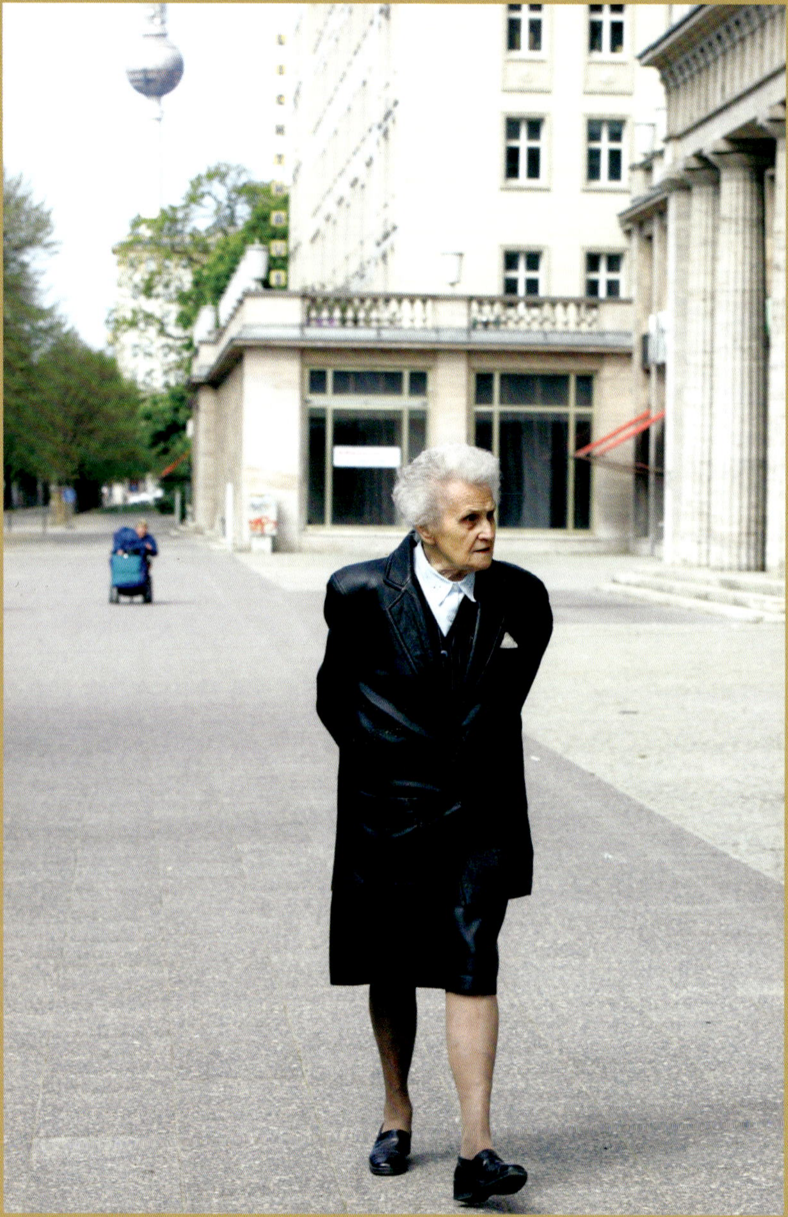

Karl-Marx-Allee

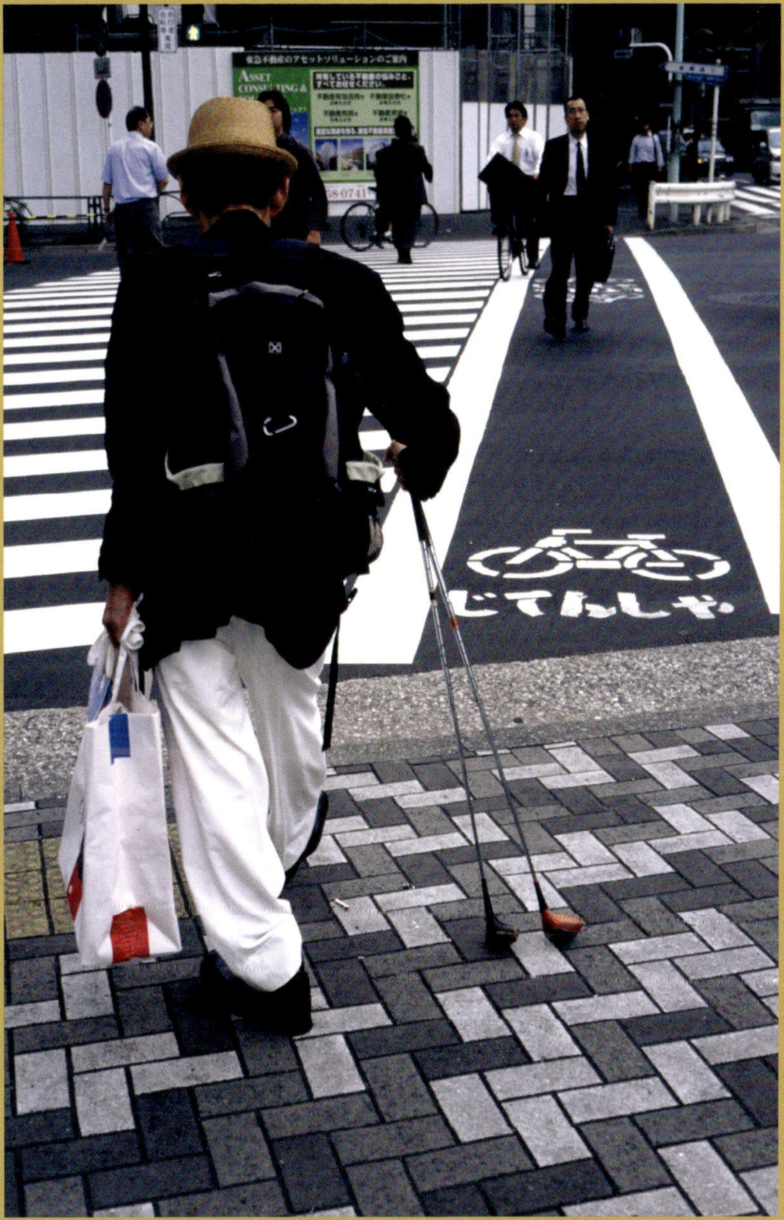

Kanda

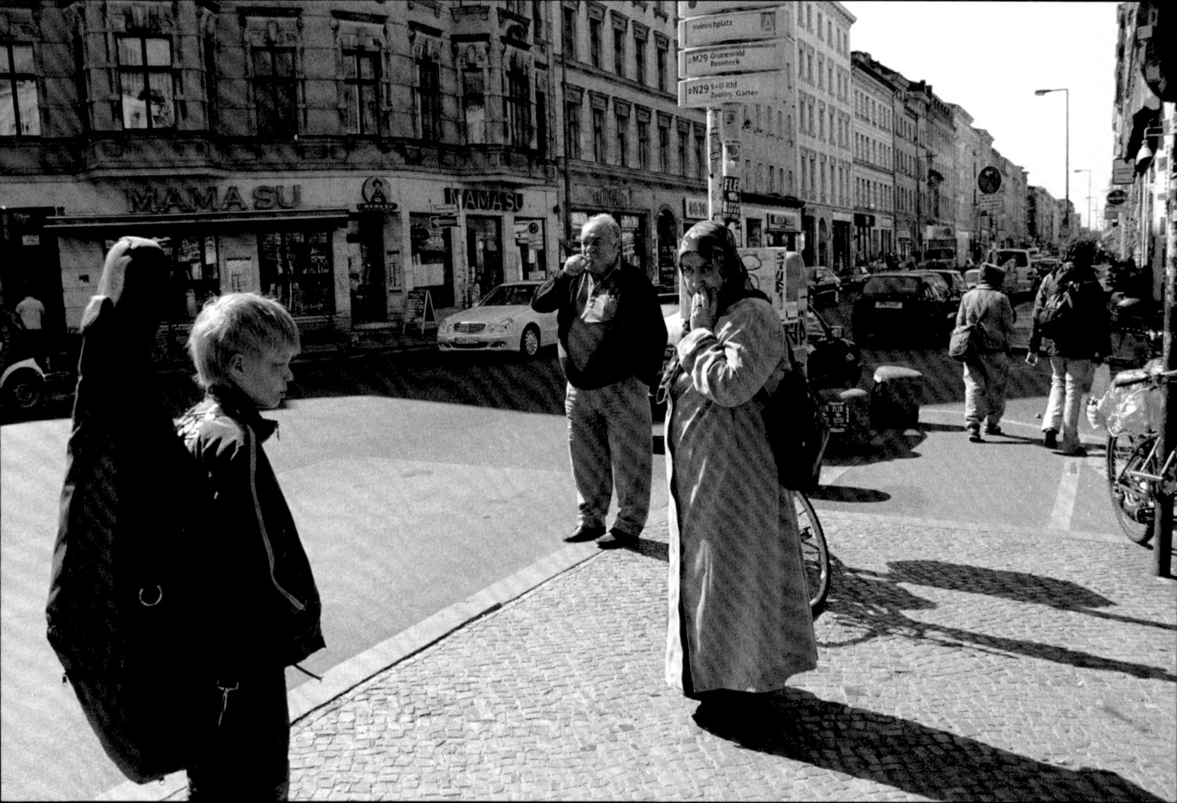
Heinrichplatz
M29 Grunewald Roseneck
N29 S+U-Bhf Zoolog. Garten
MAMASU
MAMASU

Kreuzberg

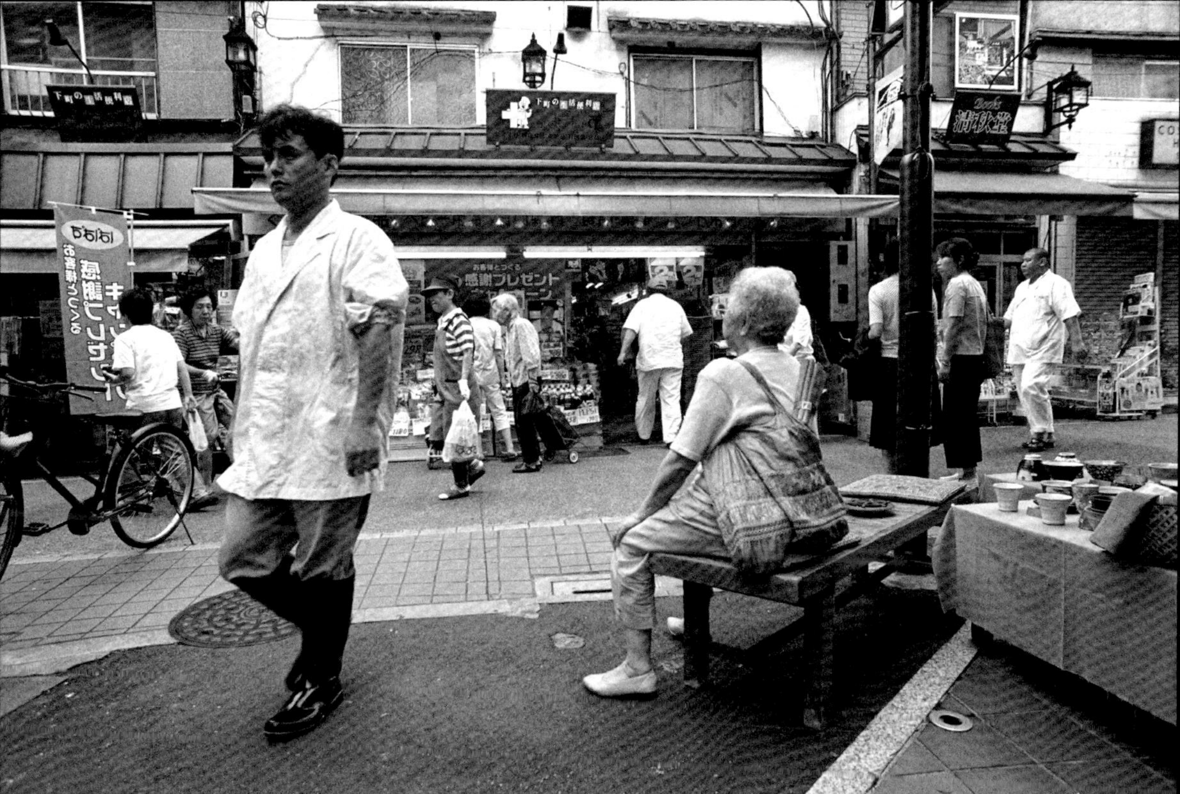

Yanaka

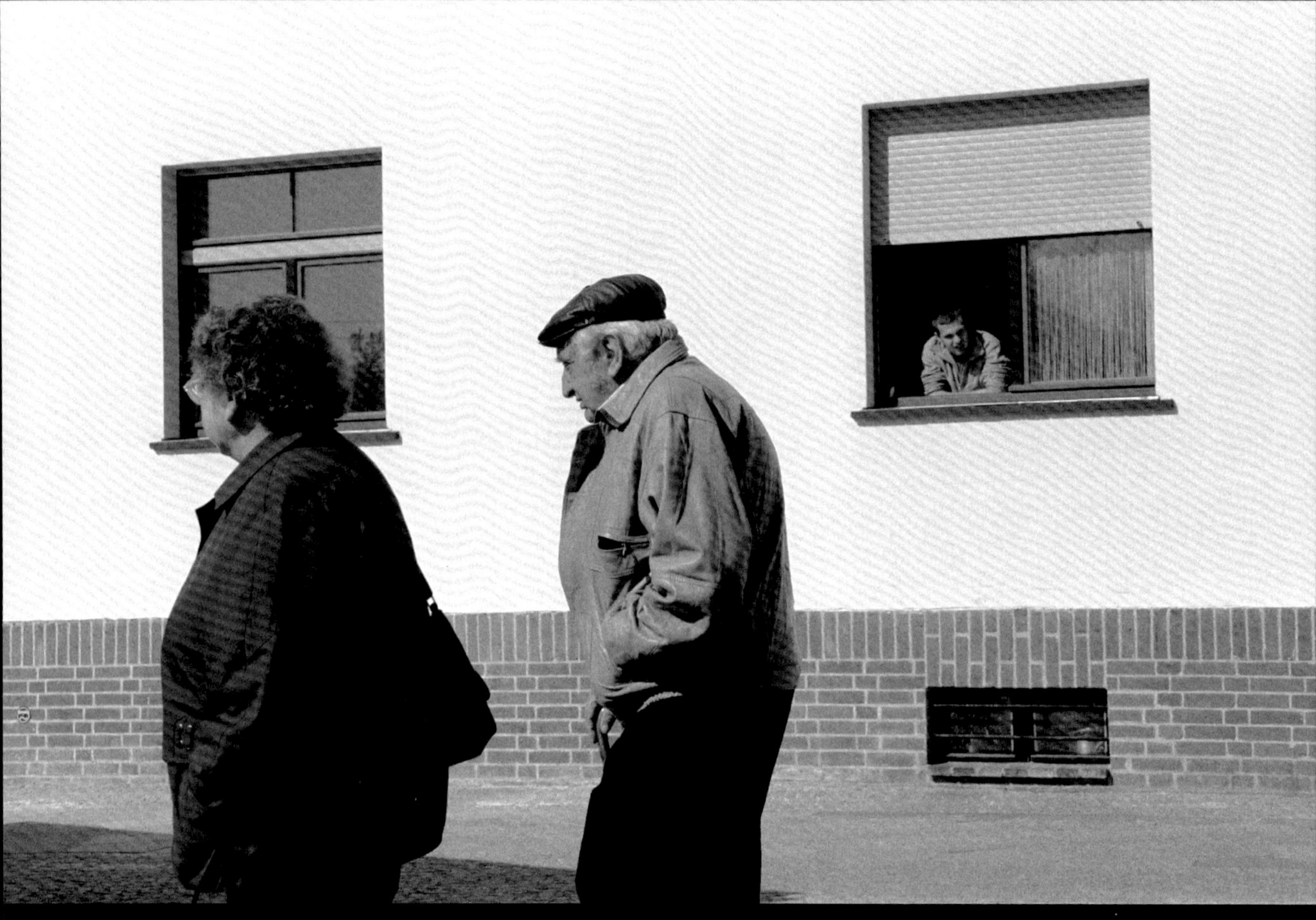

Prenzlauer Berg

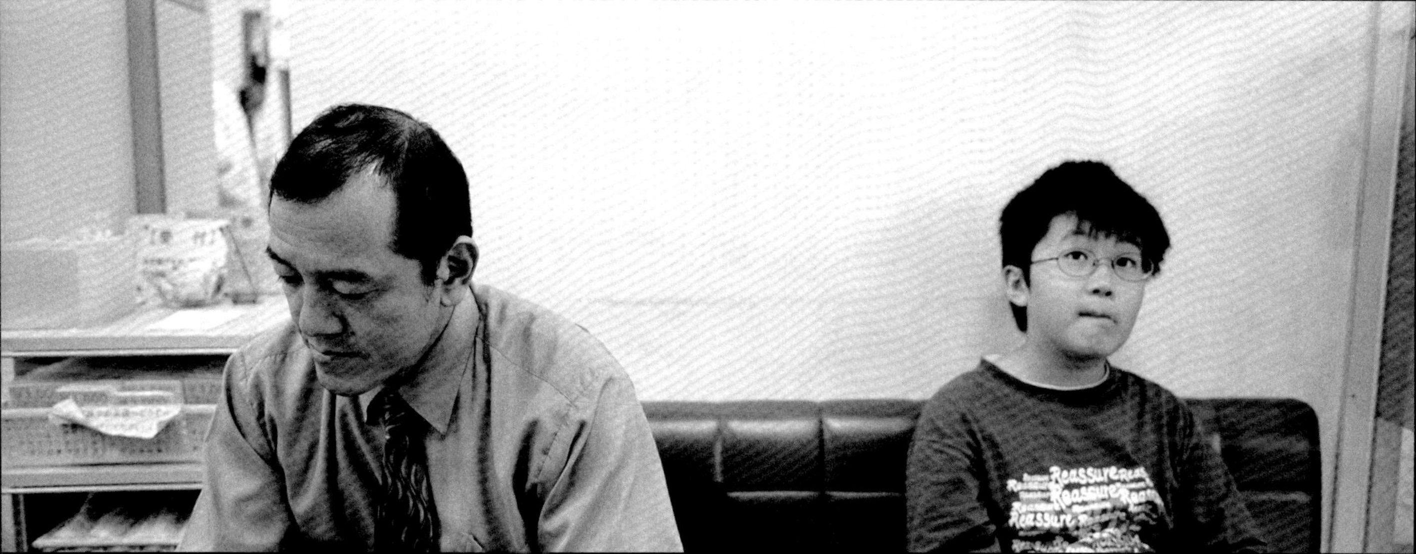

Ueno

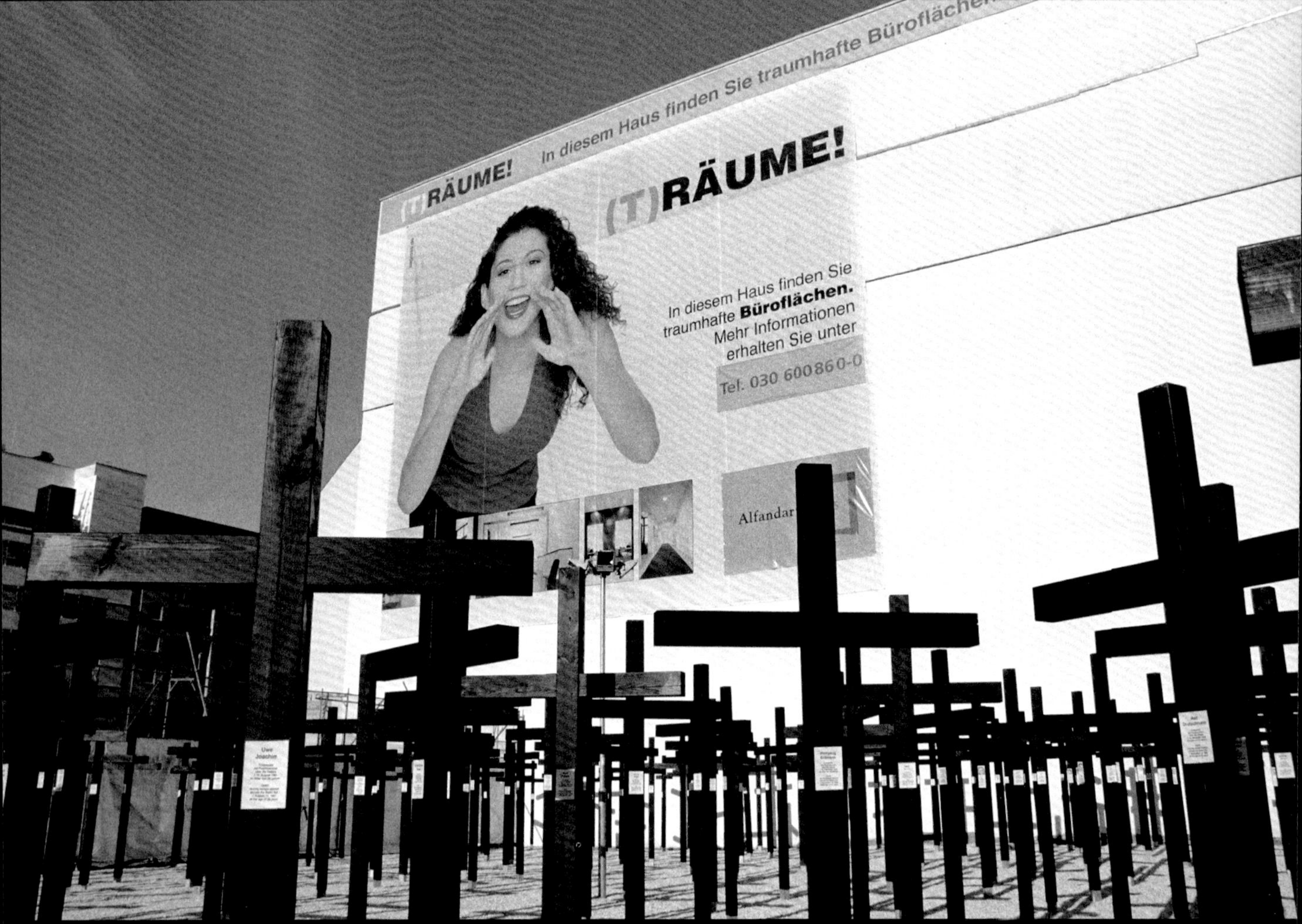

Privates Mahnmal für Maueropfer, Checkpoint Char

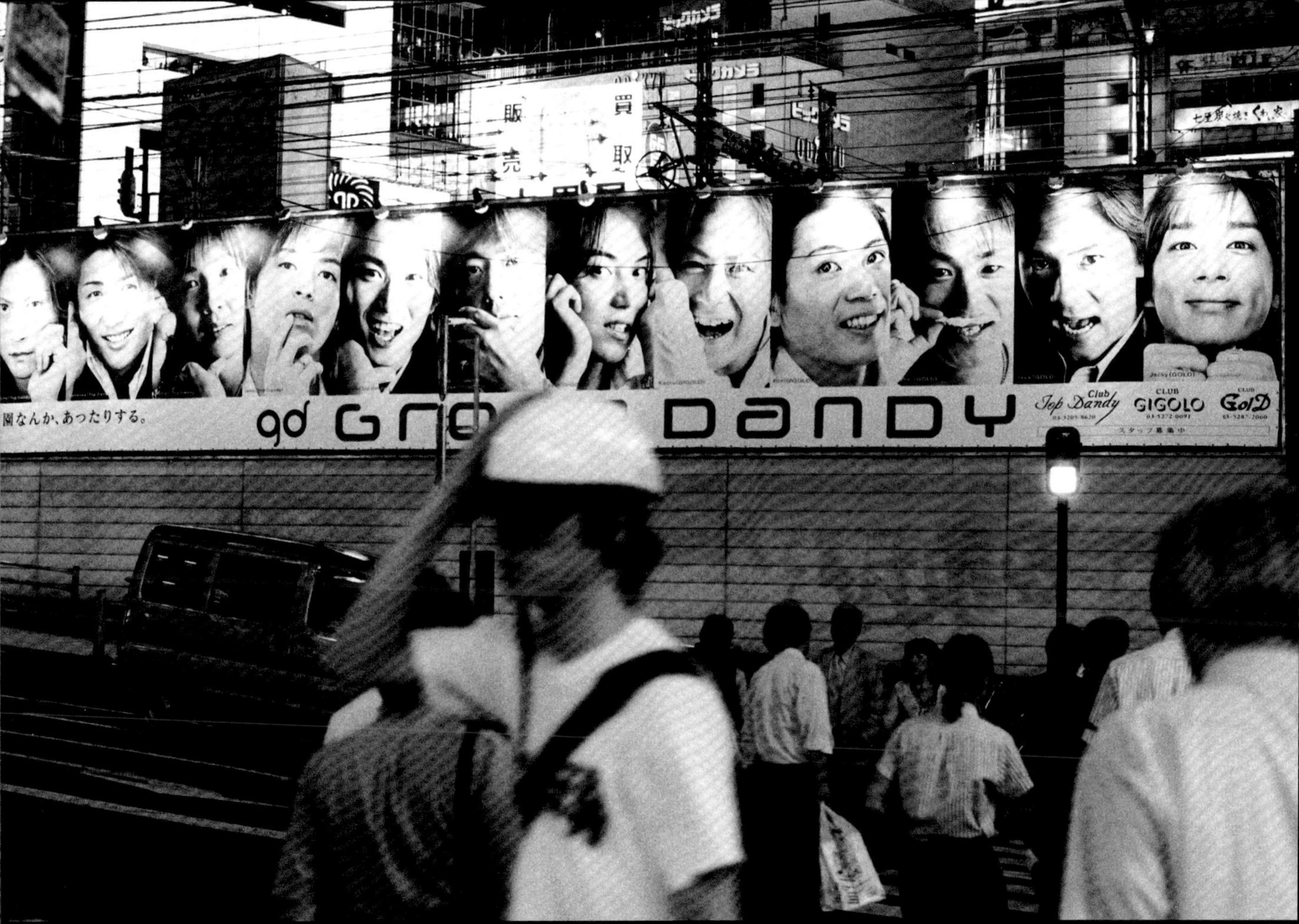
販売
買取
園なんか、あったりする。
DANDY
Club Top Dandy
CLUB GIGOLO
CLUB GolD
スタッフ募集中

Shinjyuku

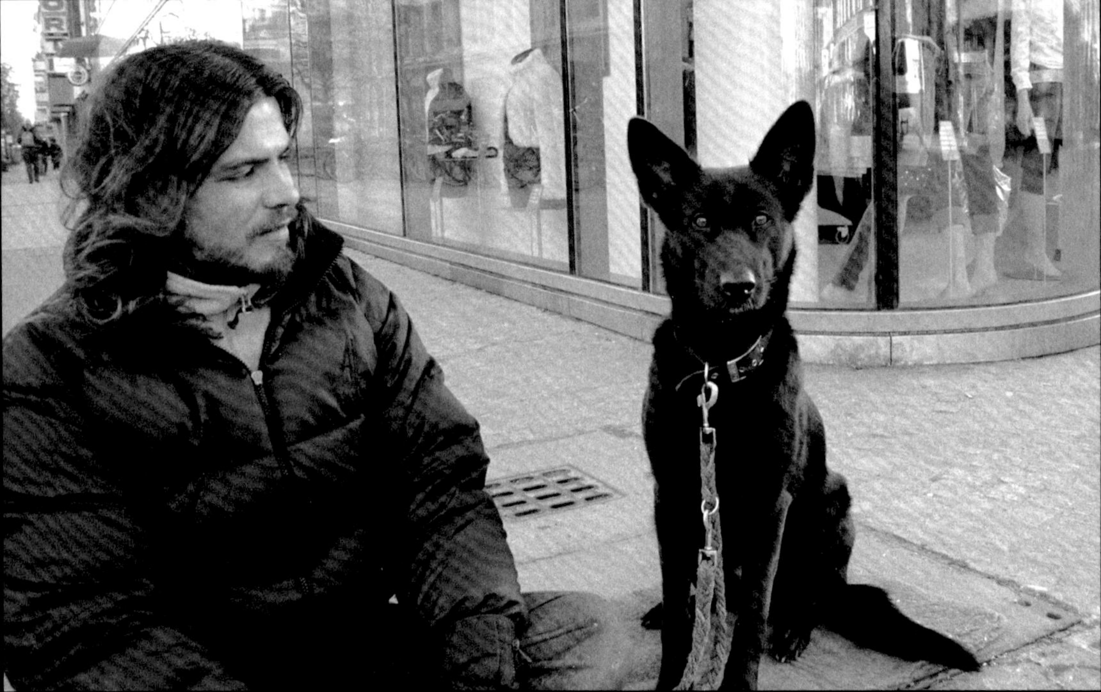

Wilmersdorfer Straße

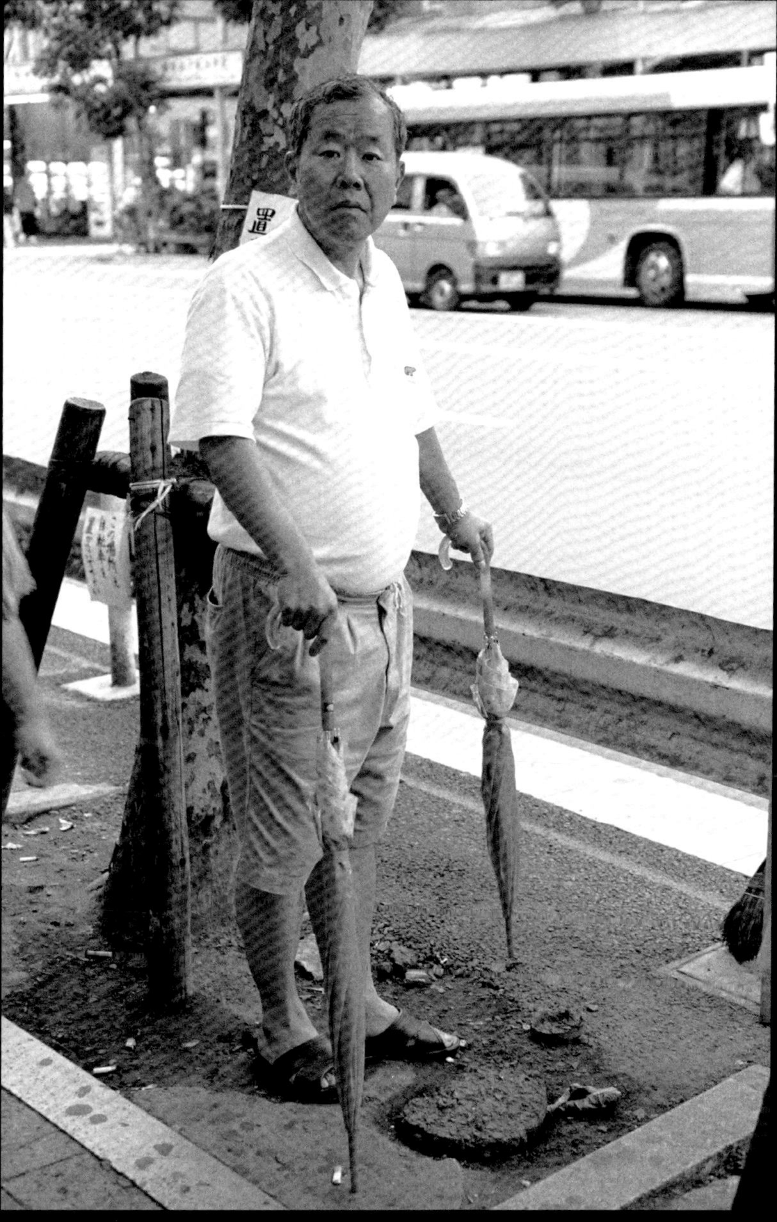

Asakusa

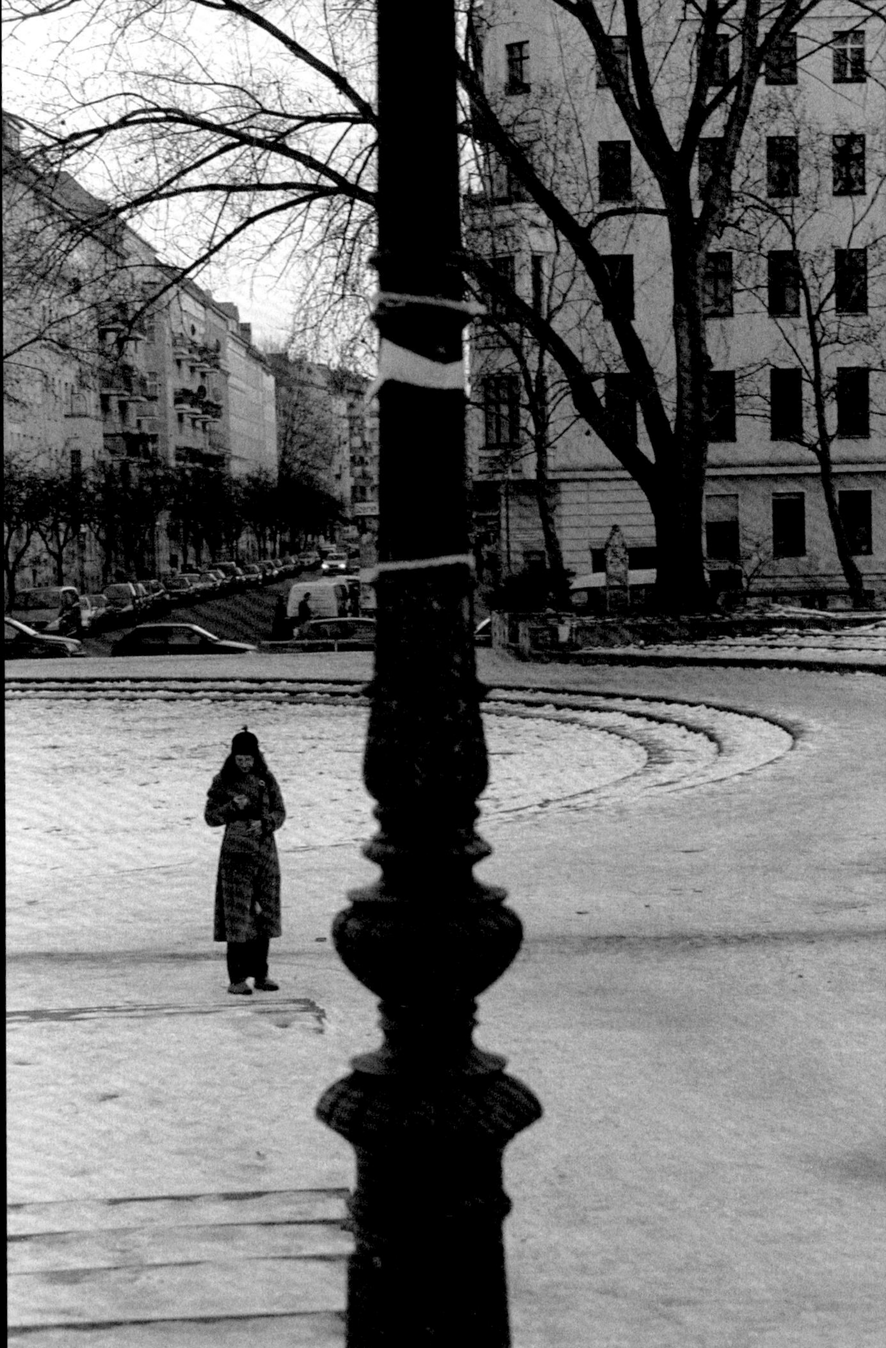

Kreuzberg

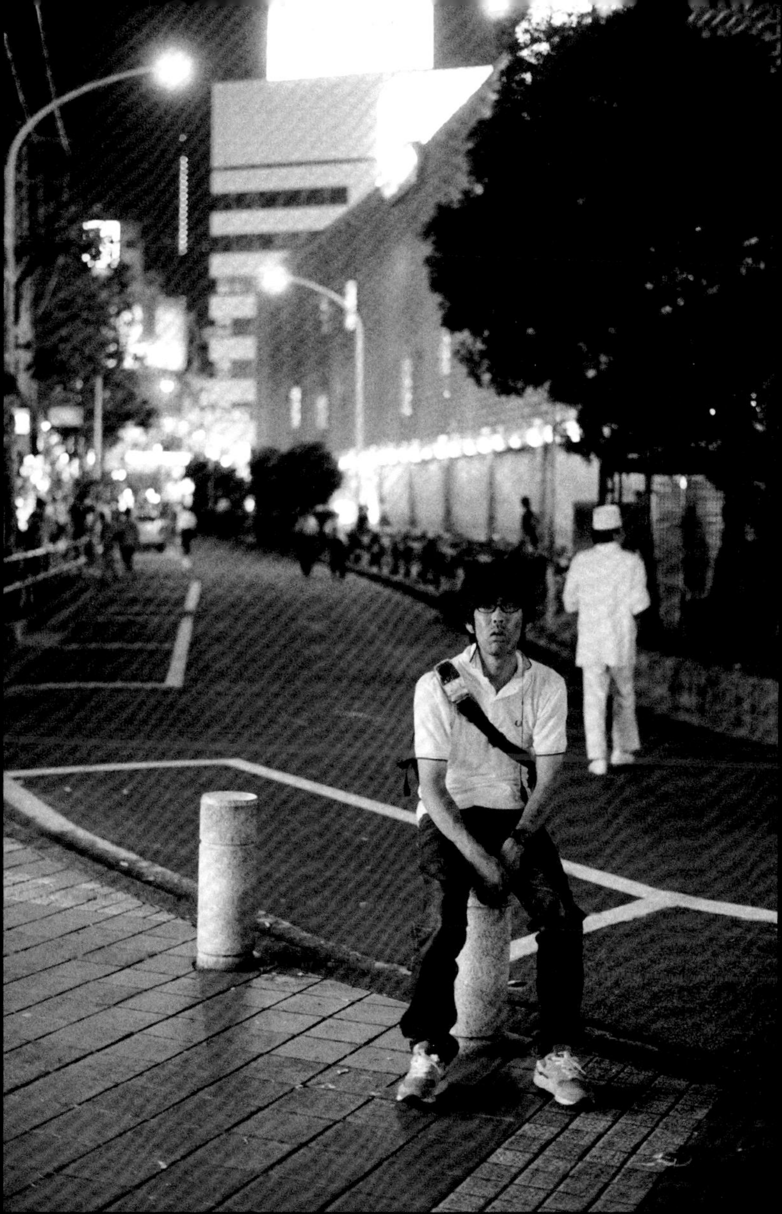

Shinbashi

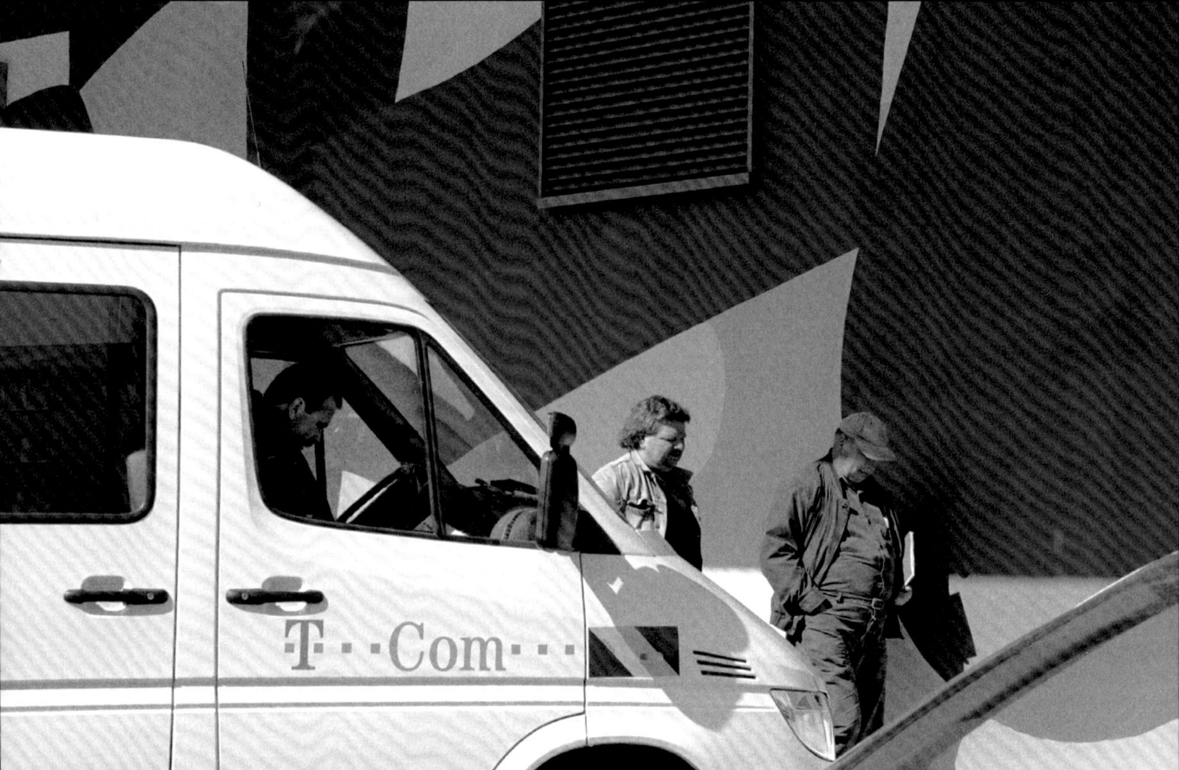

Friedrichshain

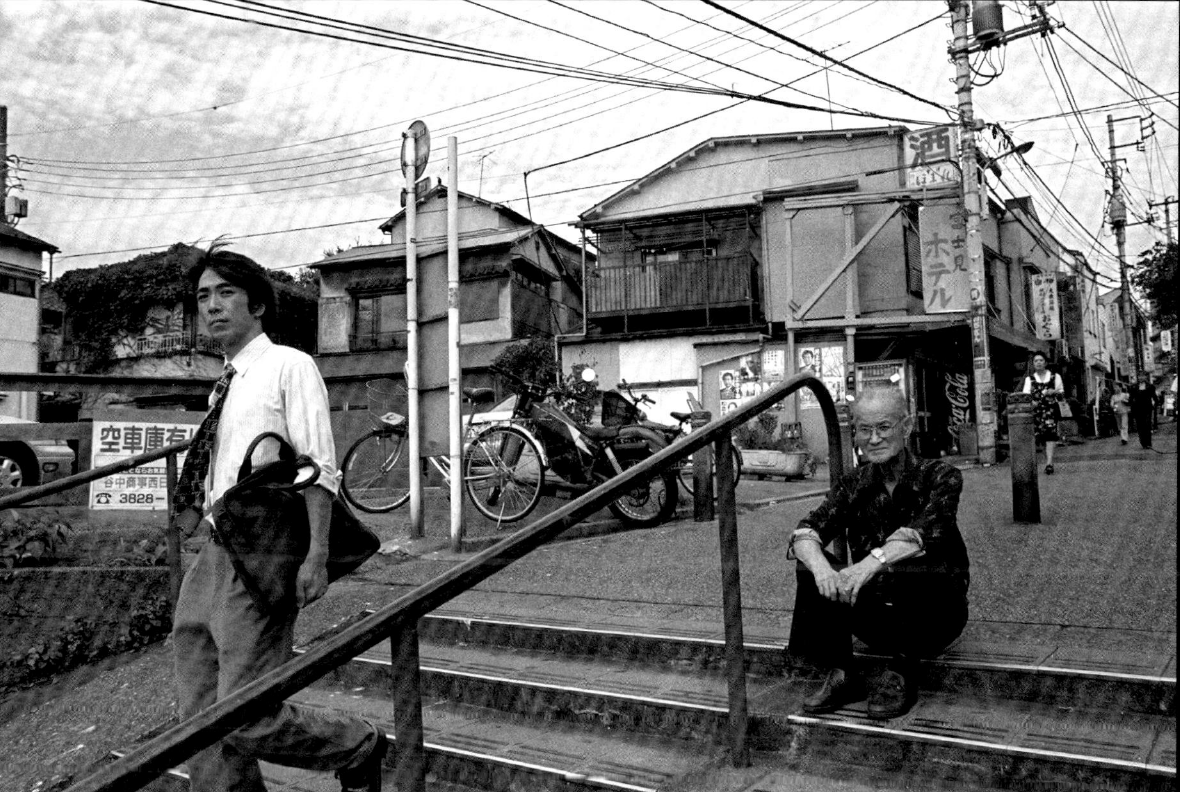

Yanaka

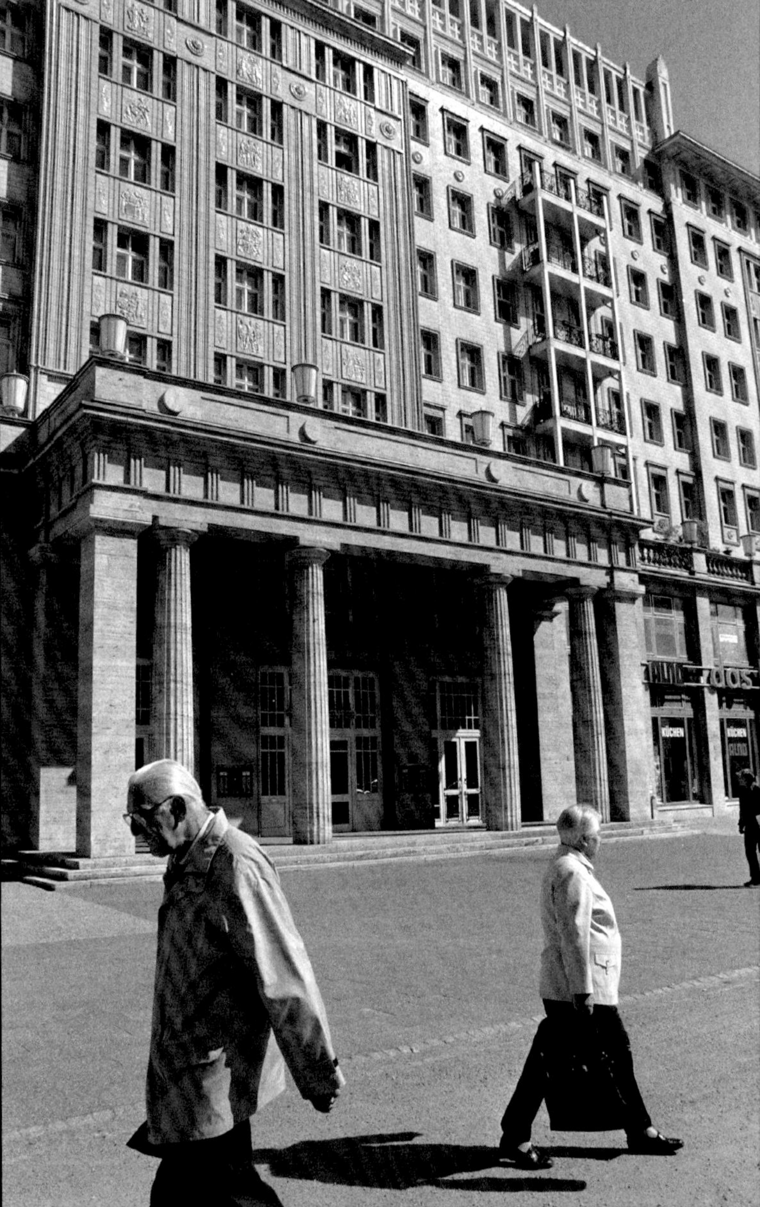

Karl-Marx-Allee

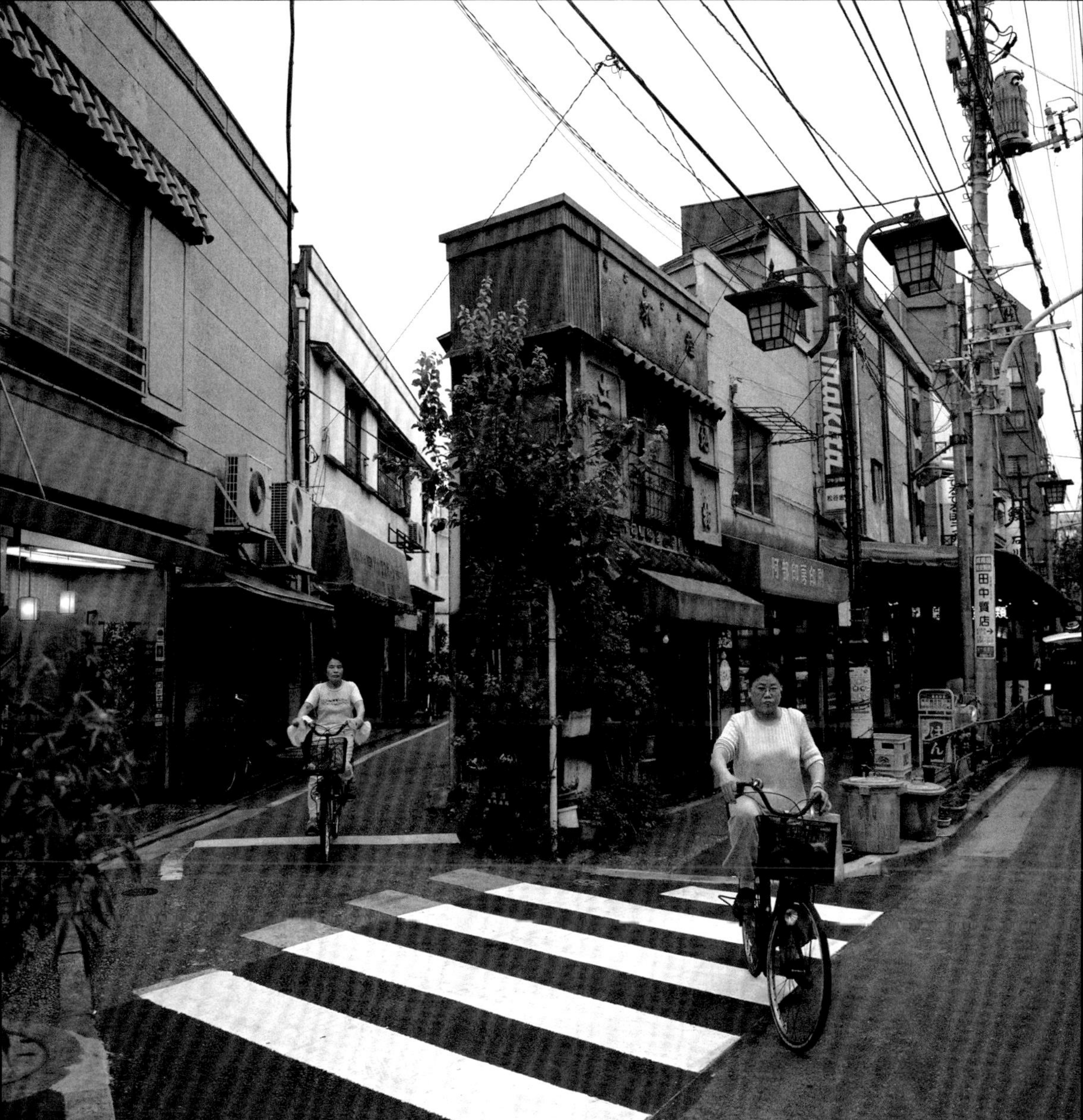

Machiya

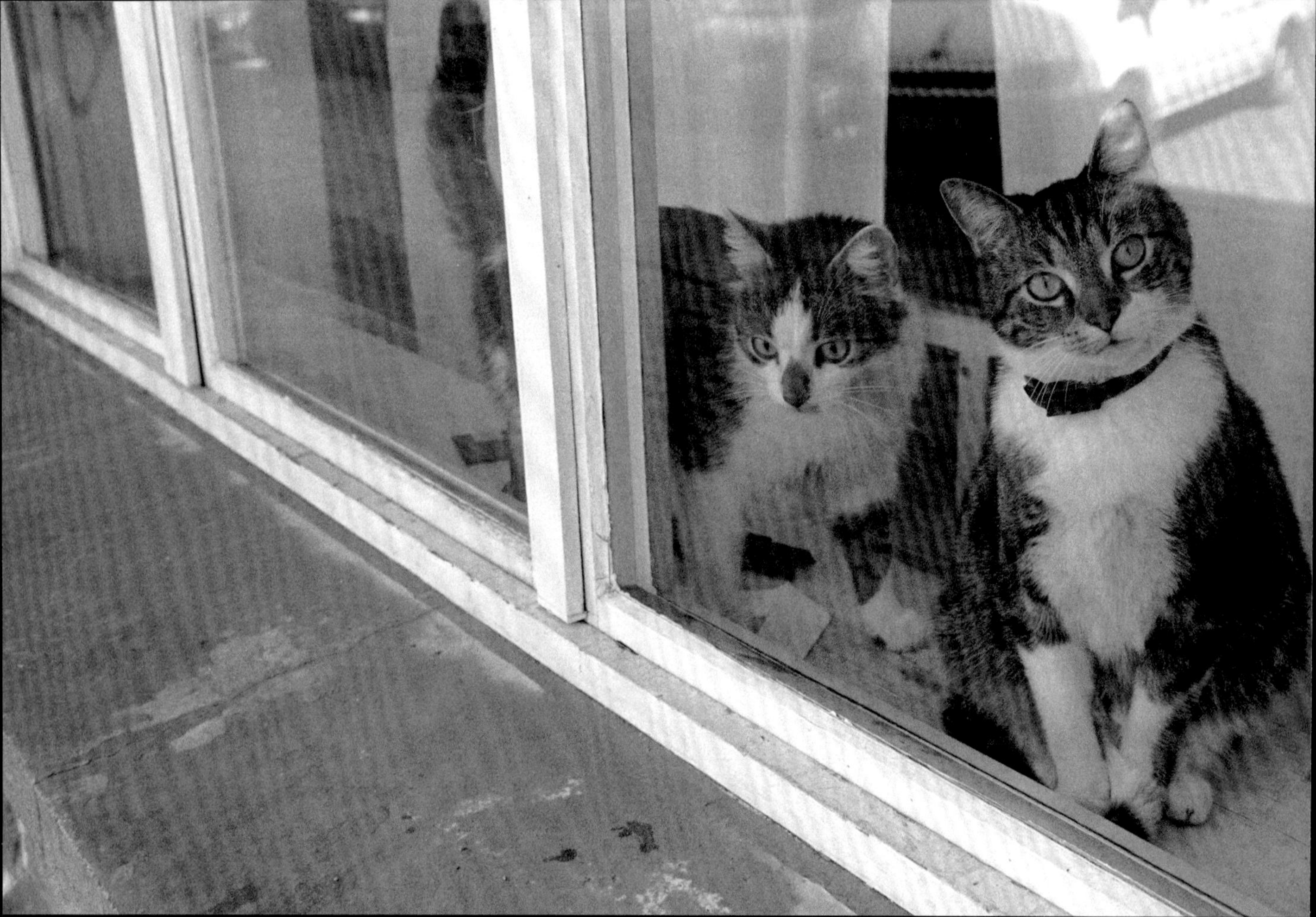

Friedrichsha

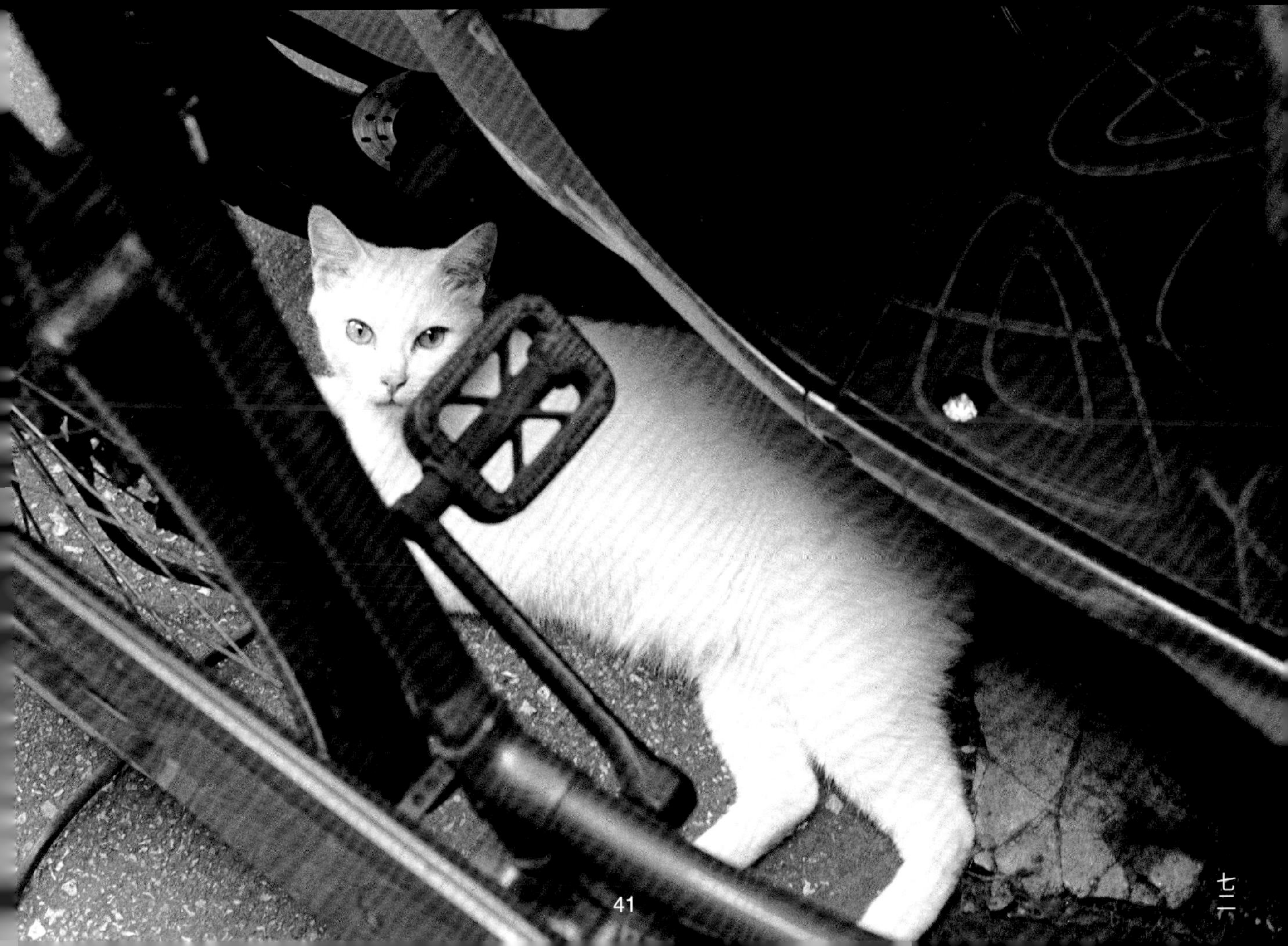

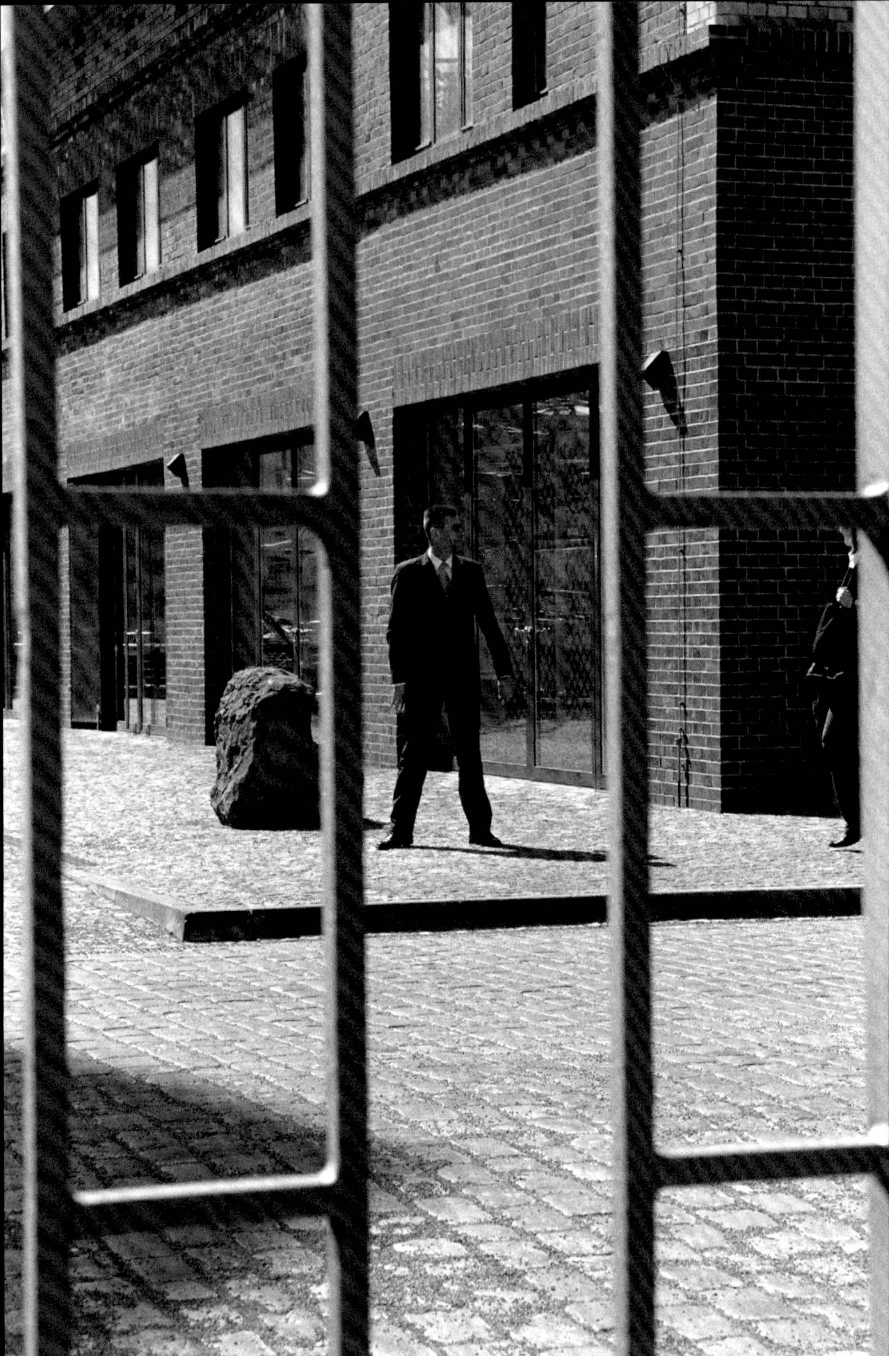

Mühlenstraße

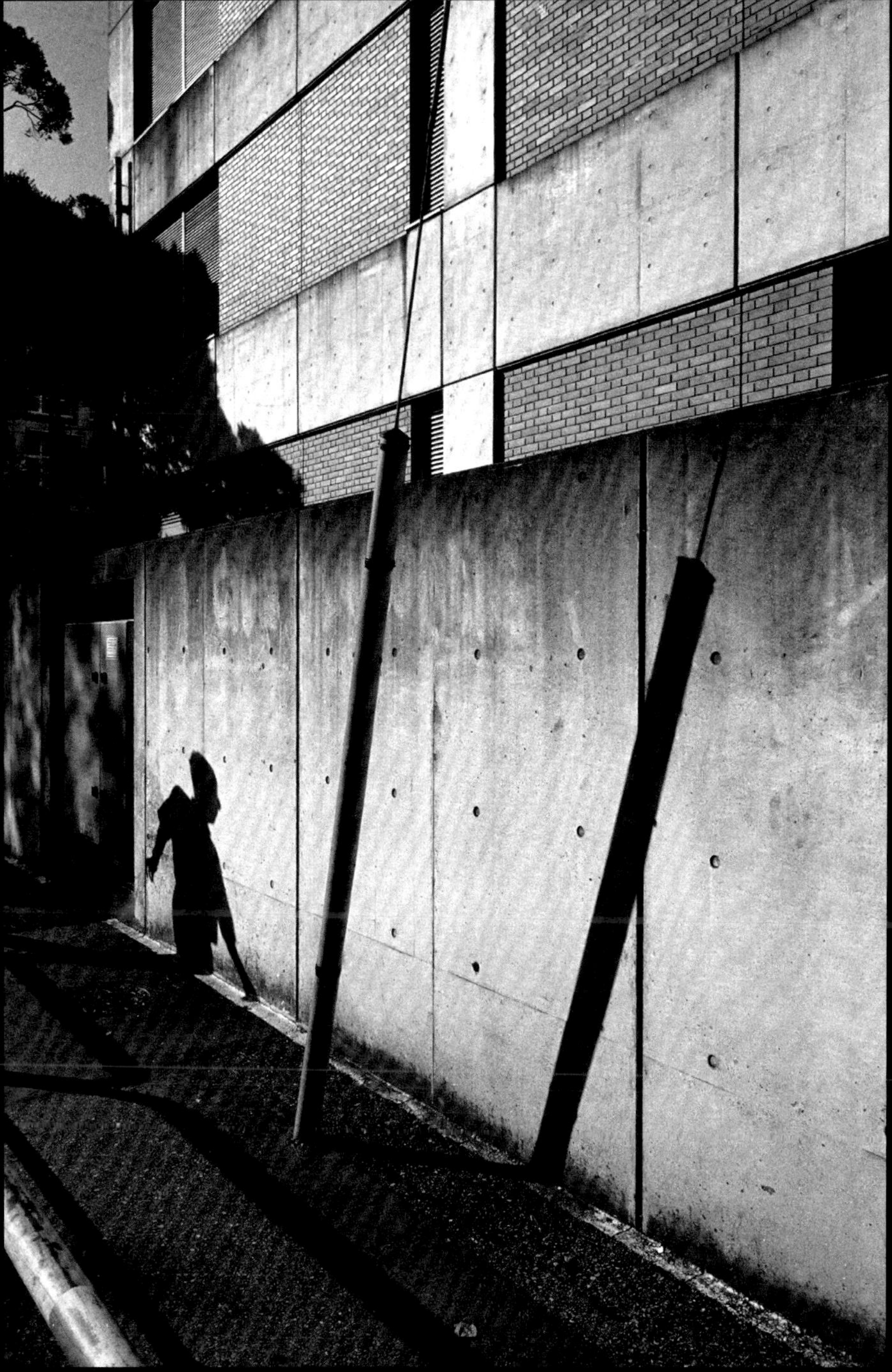

Nishinippori

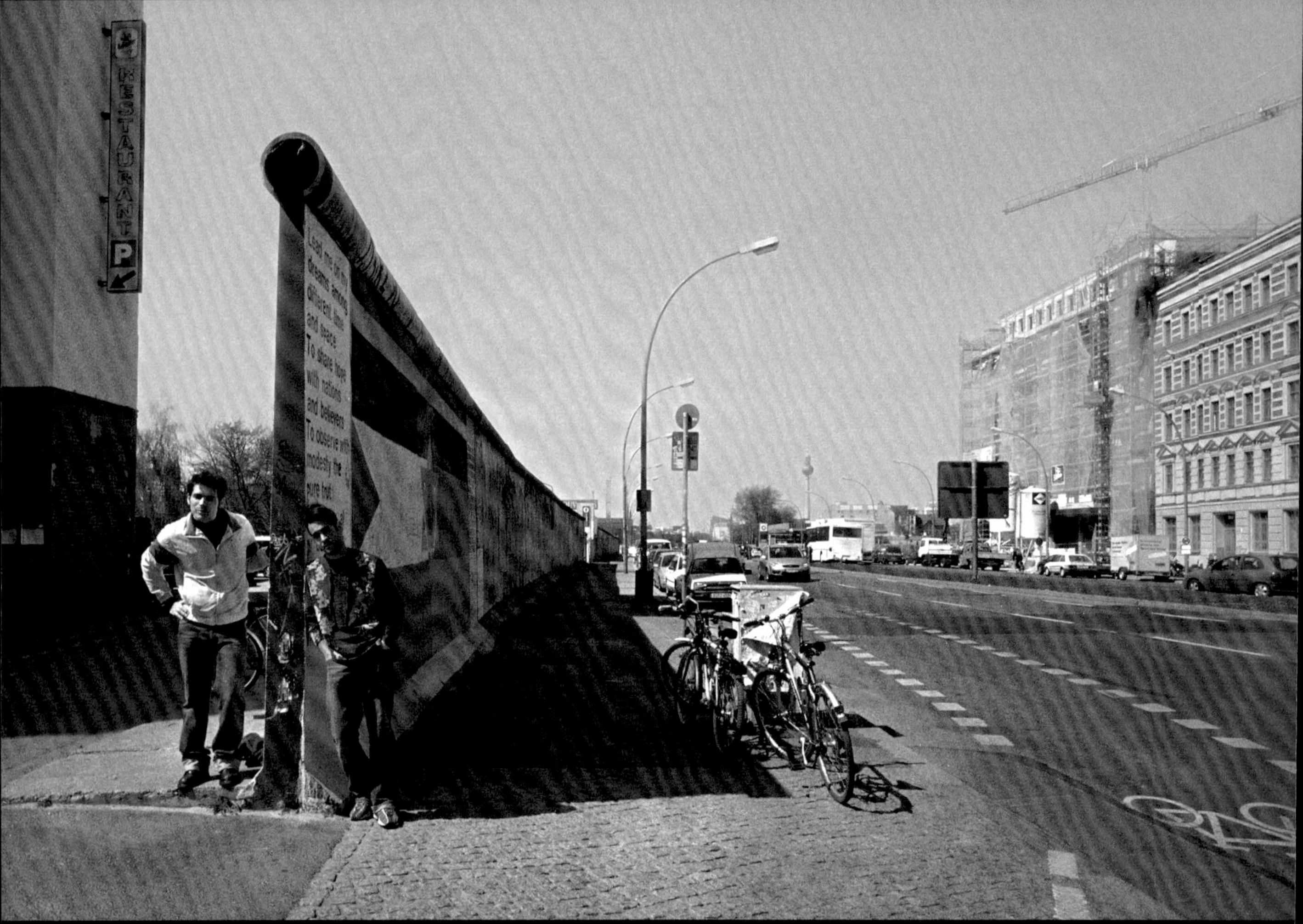

East Side Galle

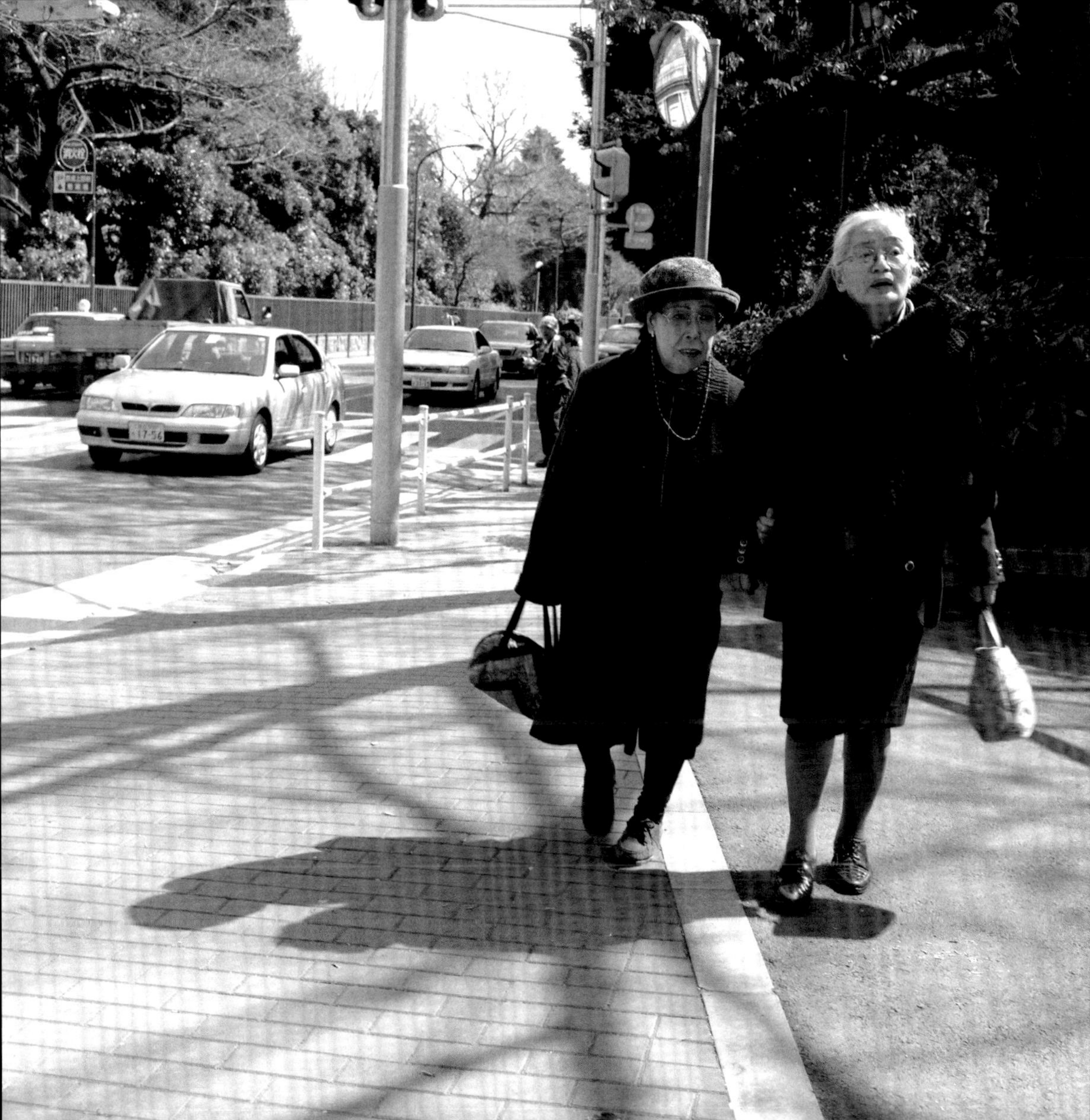

Ueno

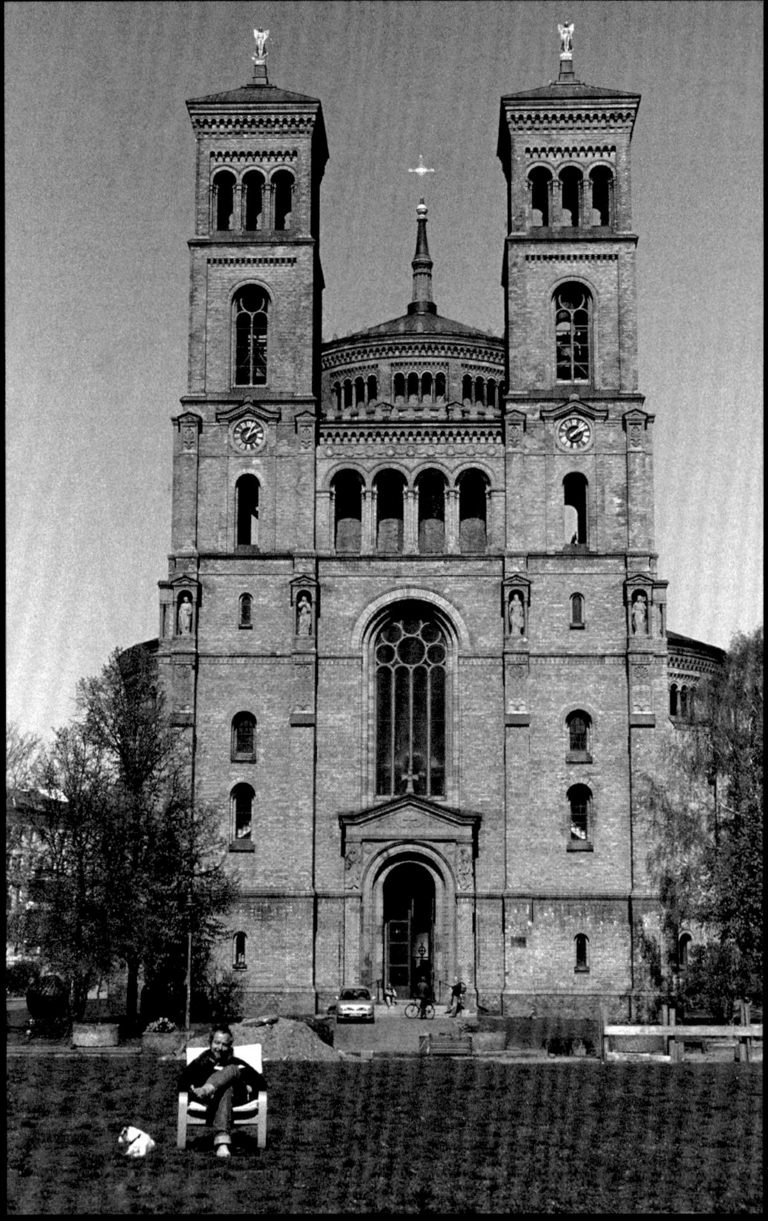

Kreuzberg

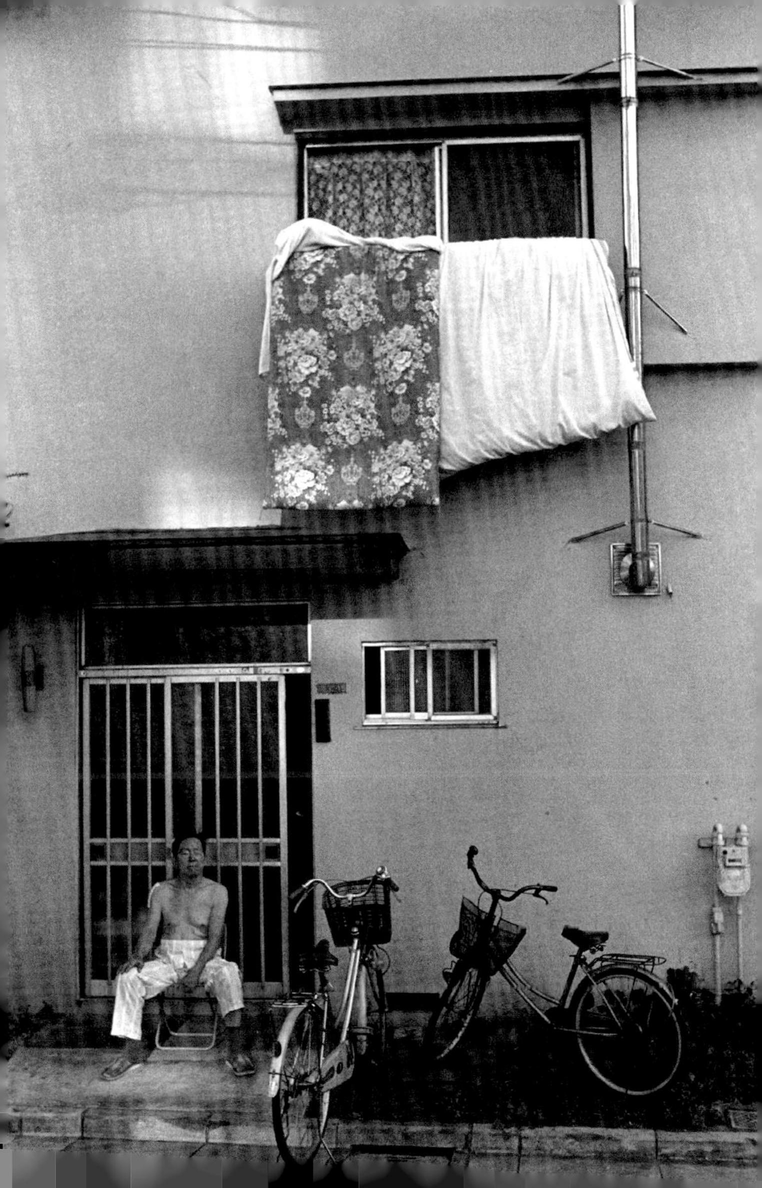

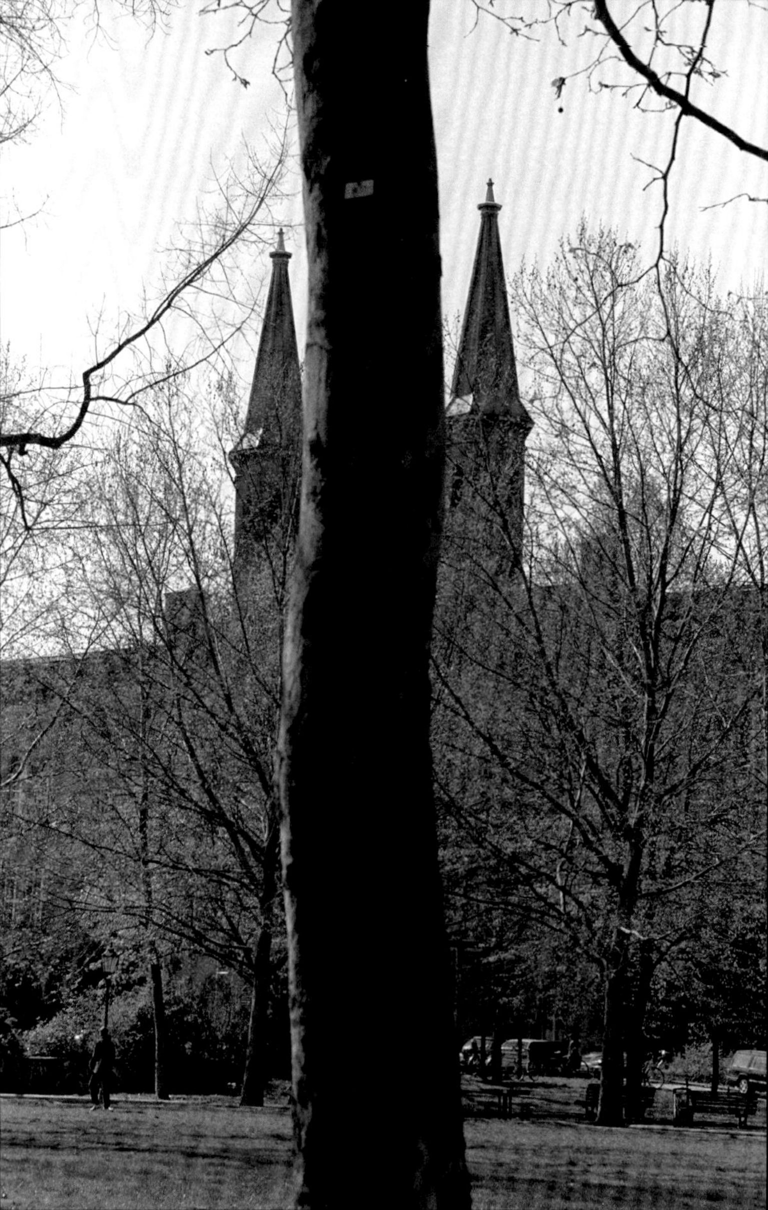

Kreuzberg

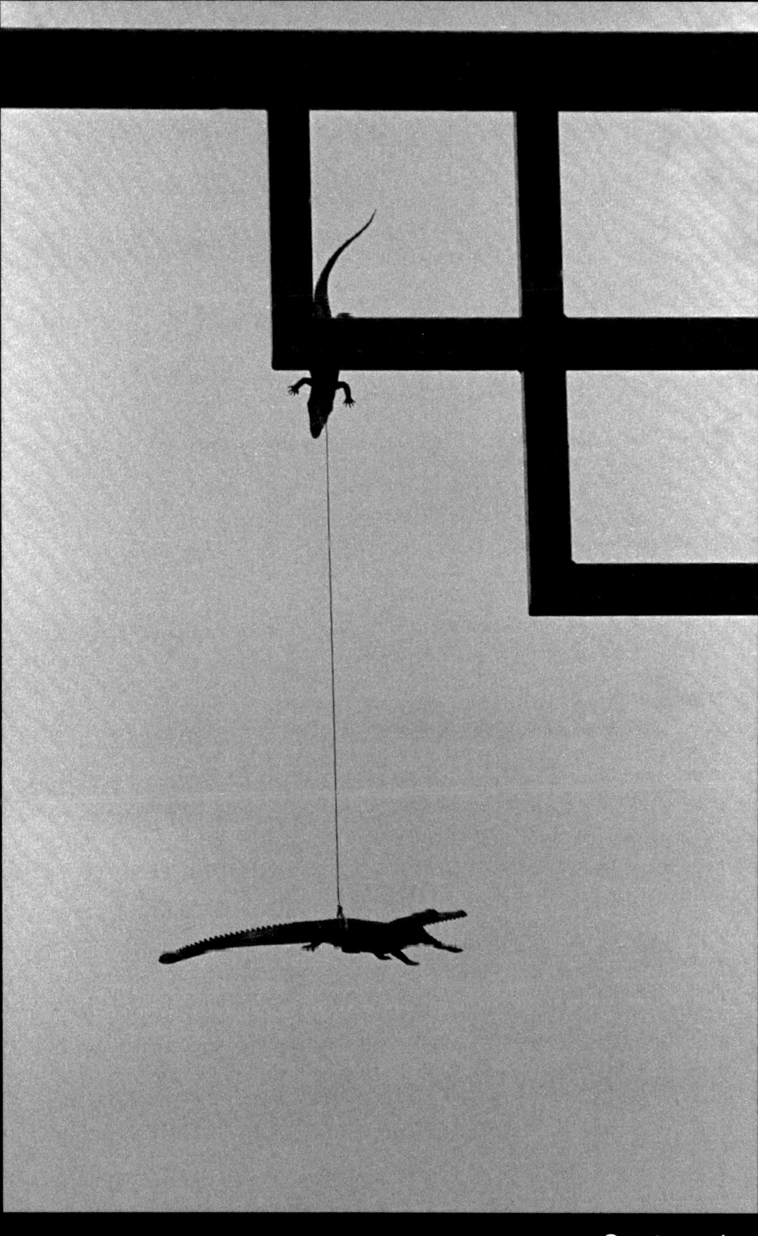

Omotesando

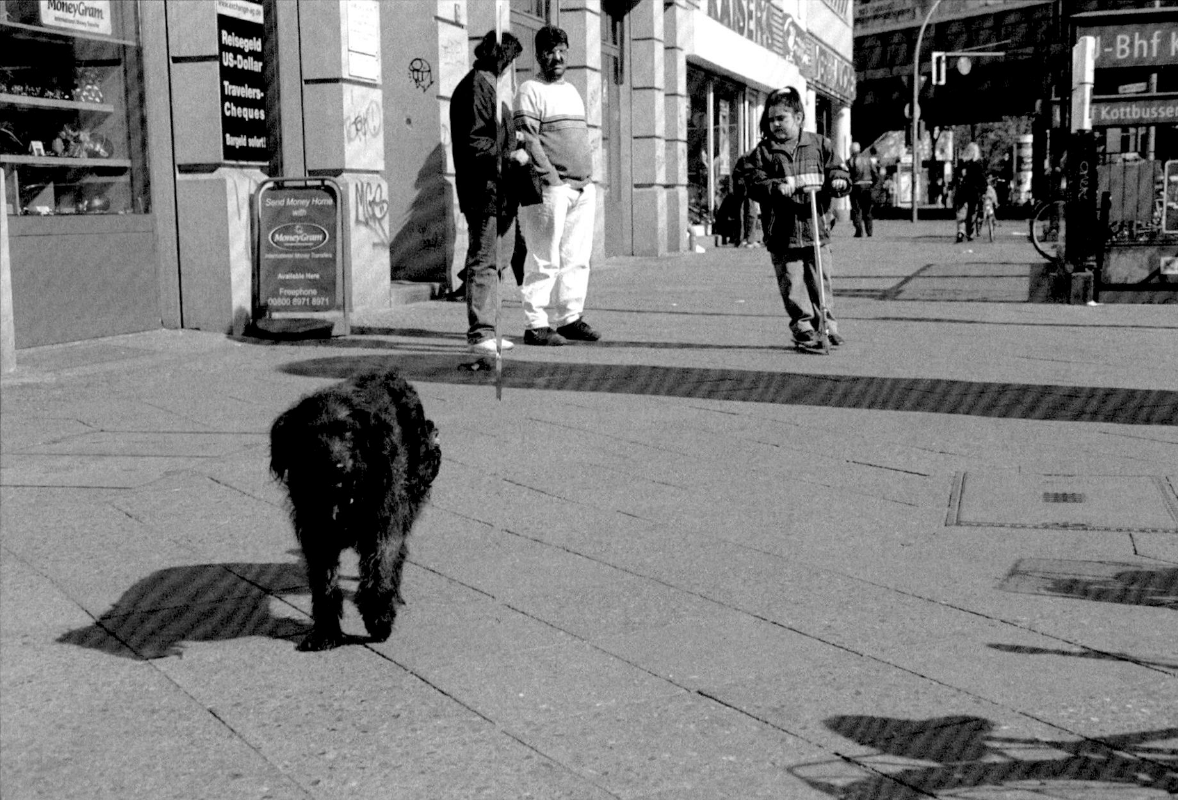
MoneyGram
Reisegeld
US-Dollar
Travelers-
Cheques
Bargeld sofort!
Send Money Home
with
MoneyGram
Available Here
Freephone
00800 8971 8971
U-Bhf K
Kottbusser

Kreuzberg

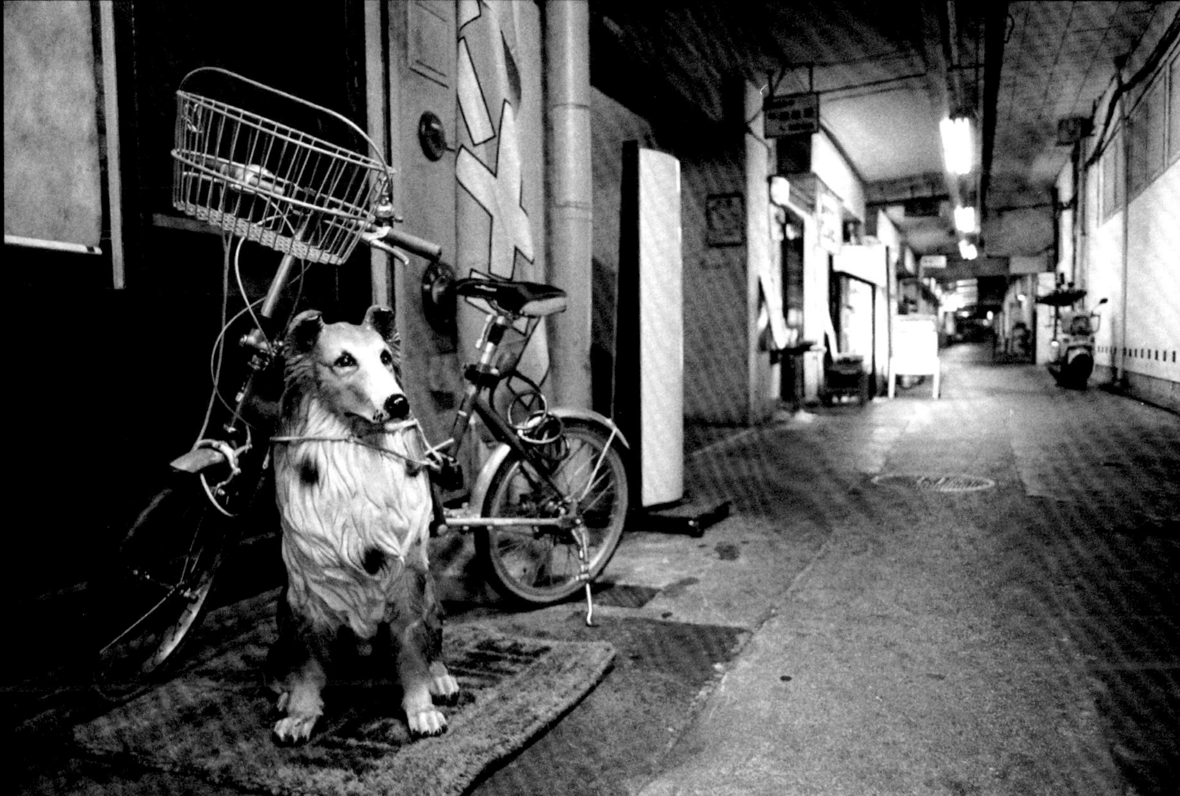

Shinbashi

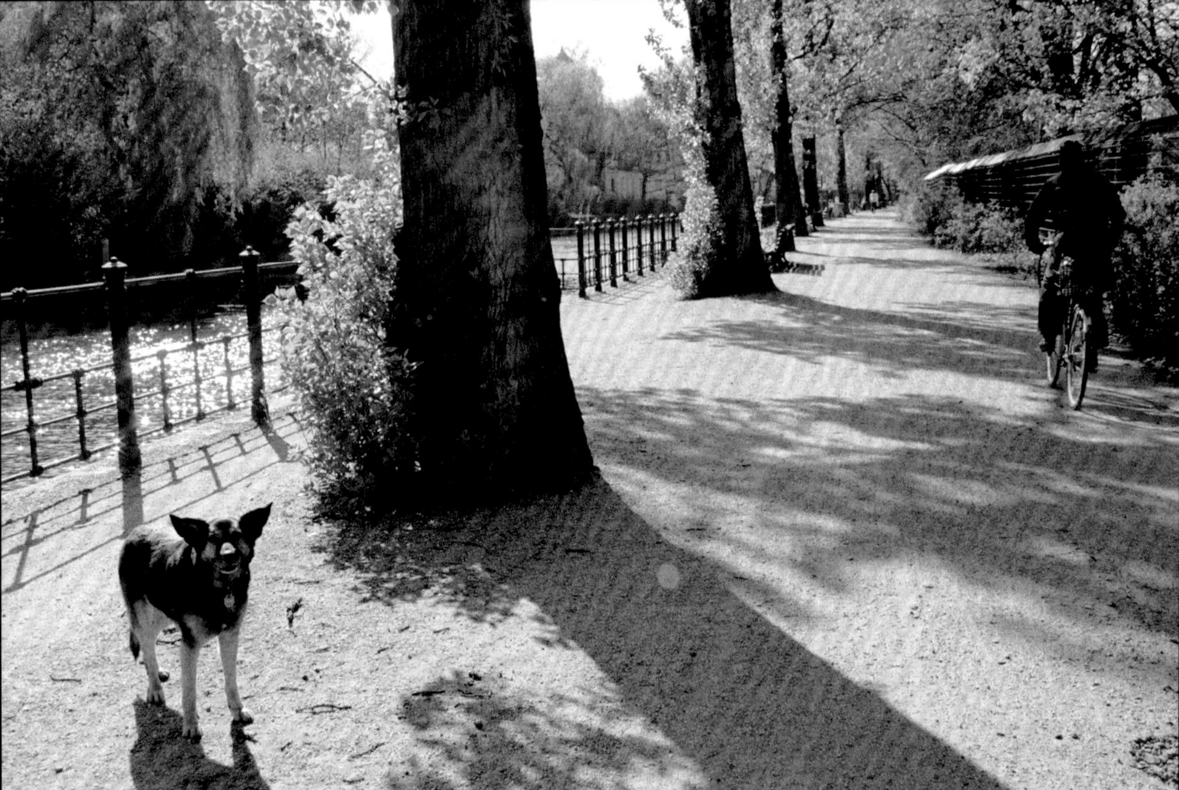

Tiergarten

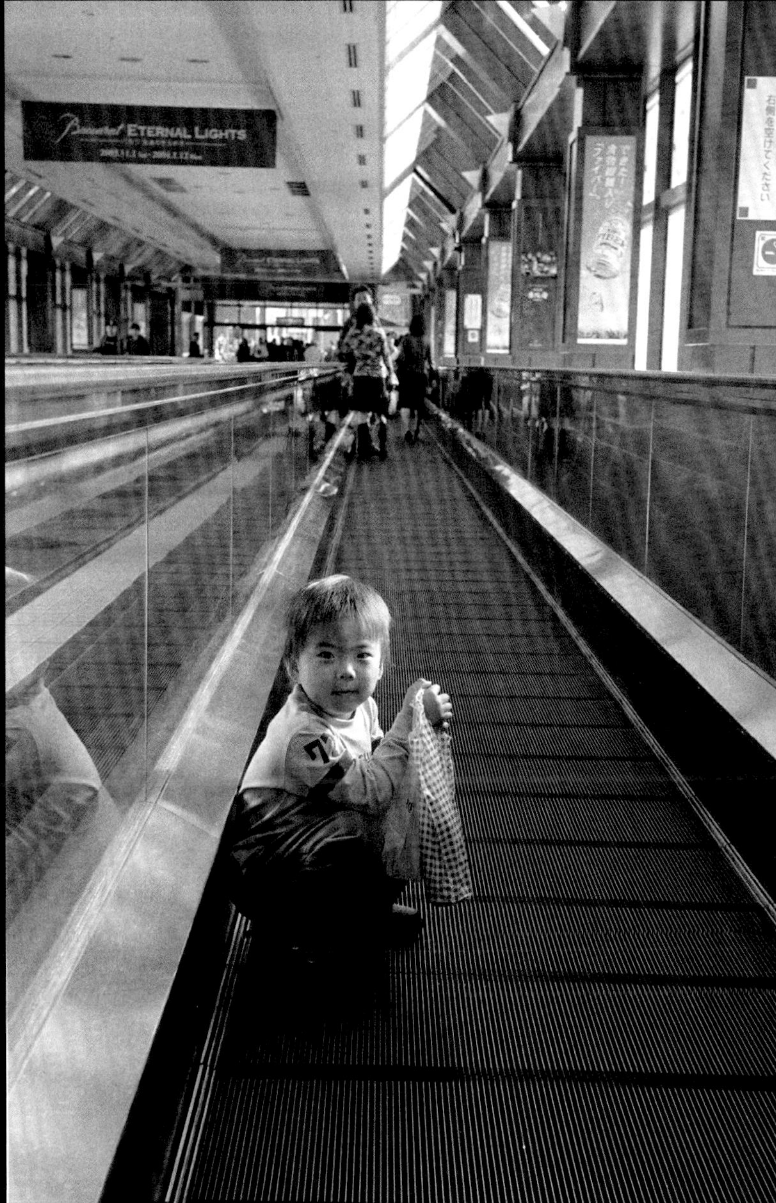

Ebisu

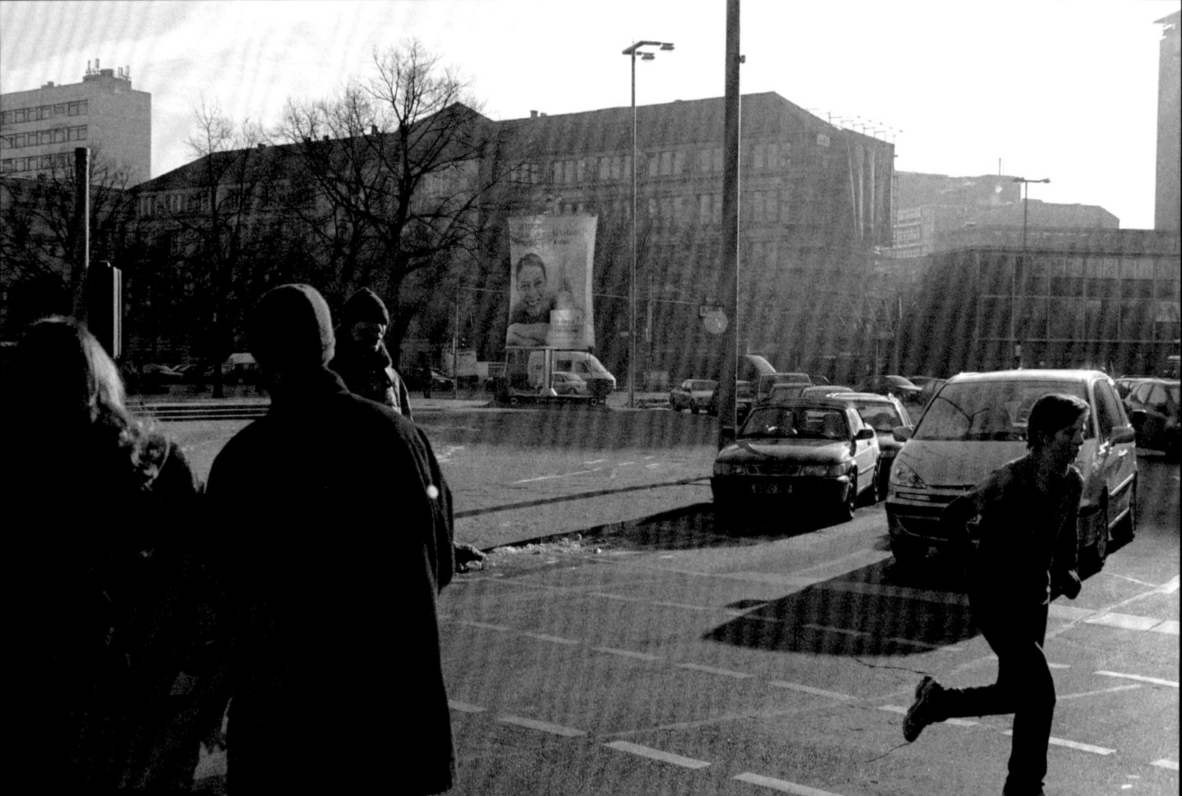

Ernst-Reuter-Platz

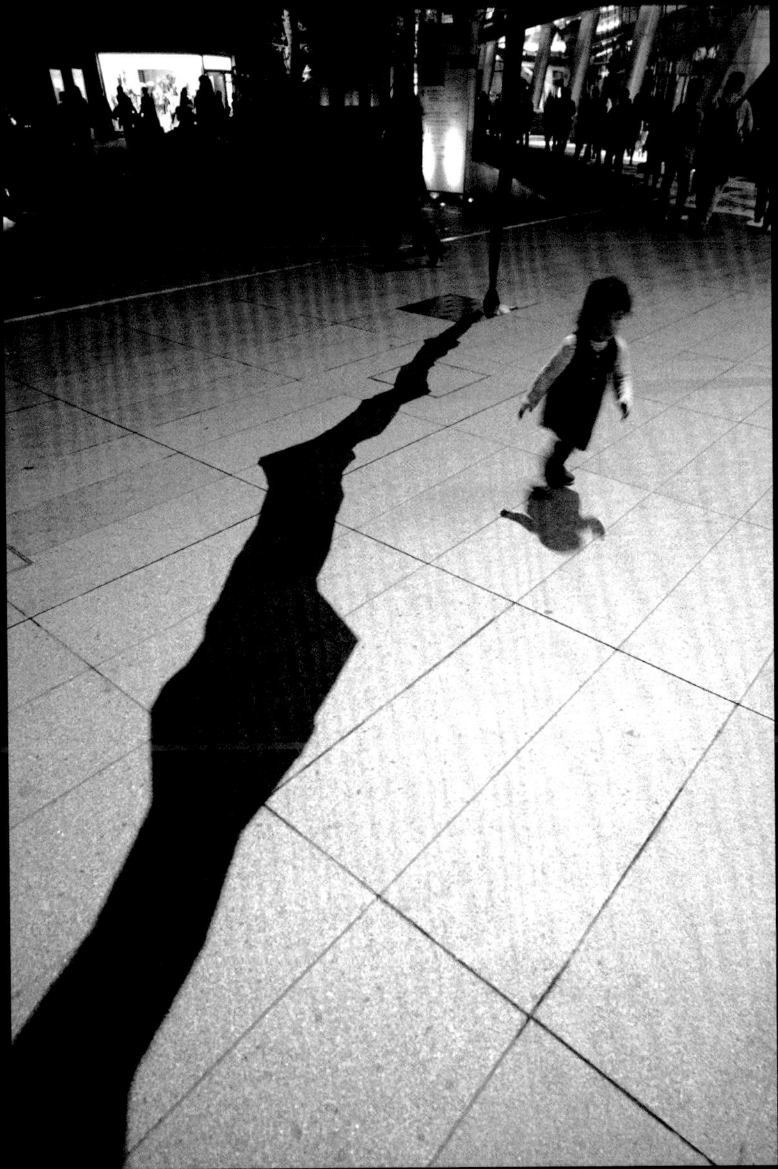

Roppongi Hills

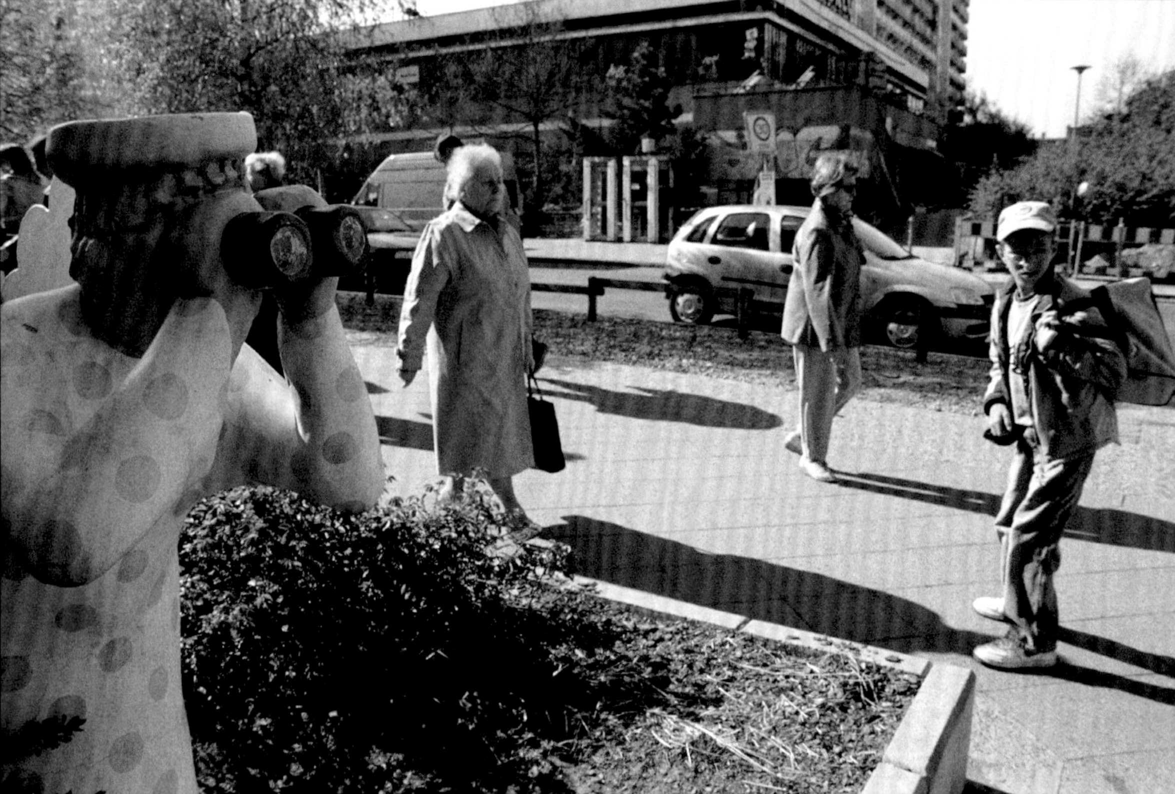

Prenzlauer Berg

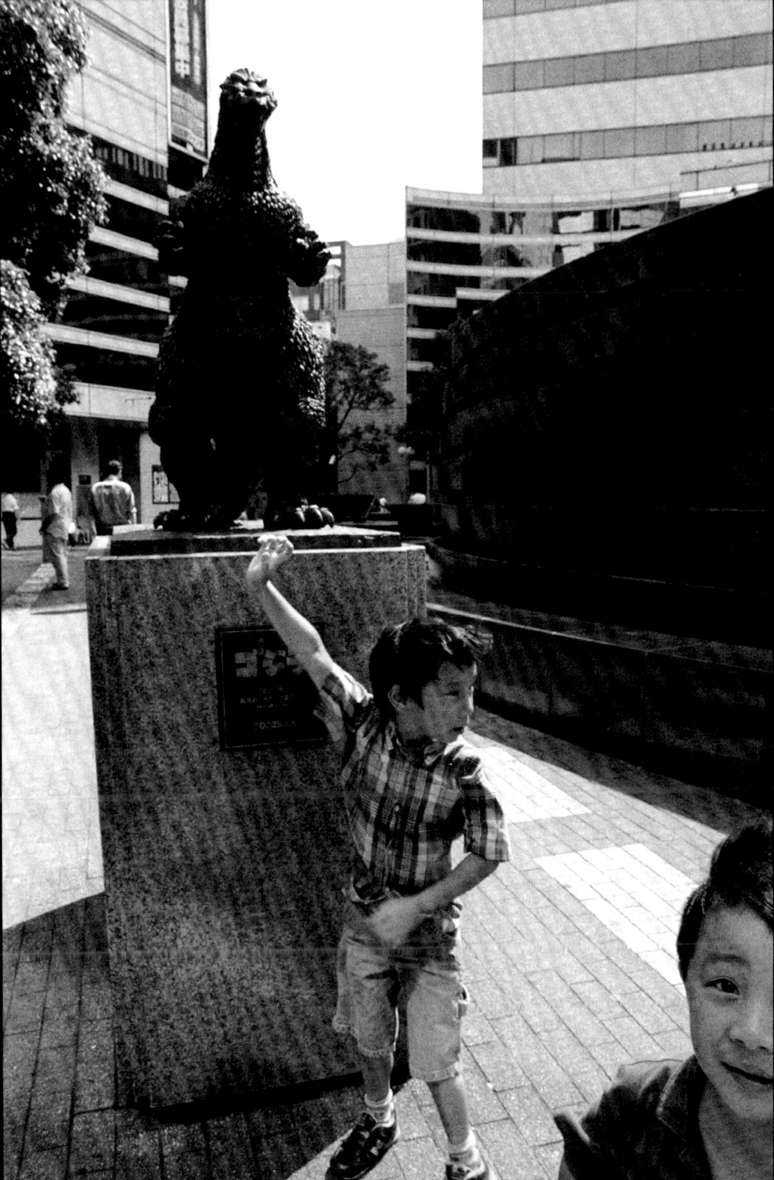

Hibiya

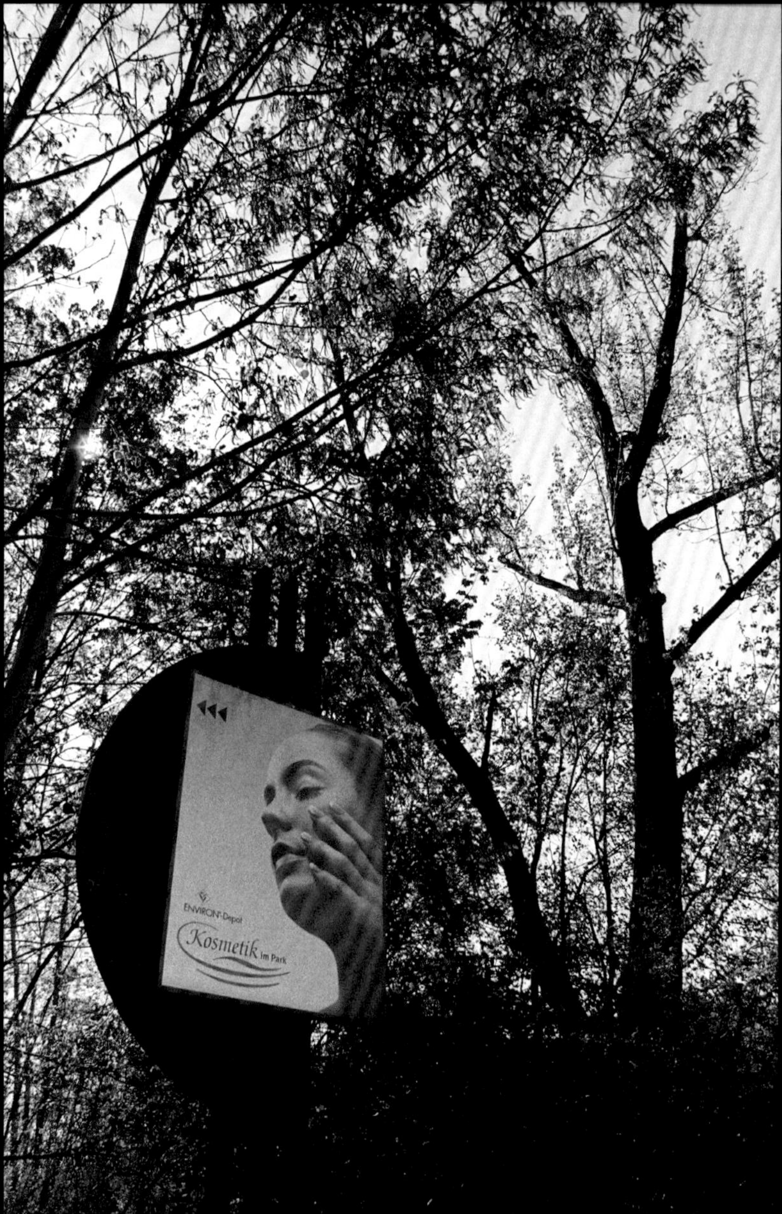

Prenzlauer Berg

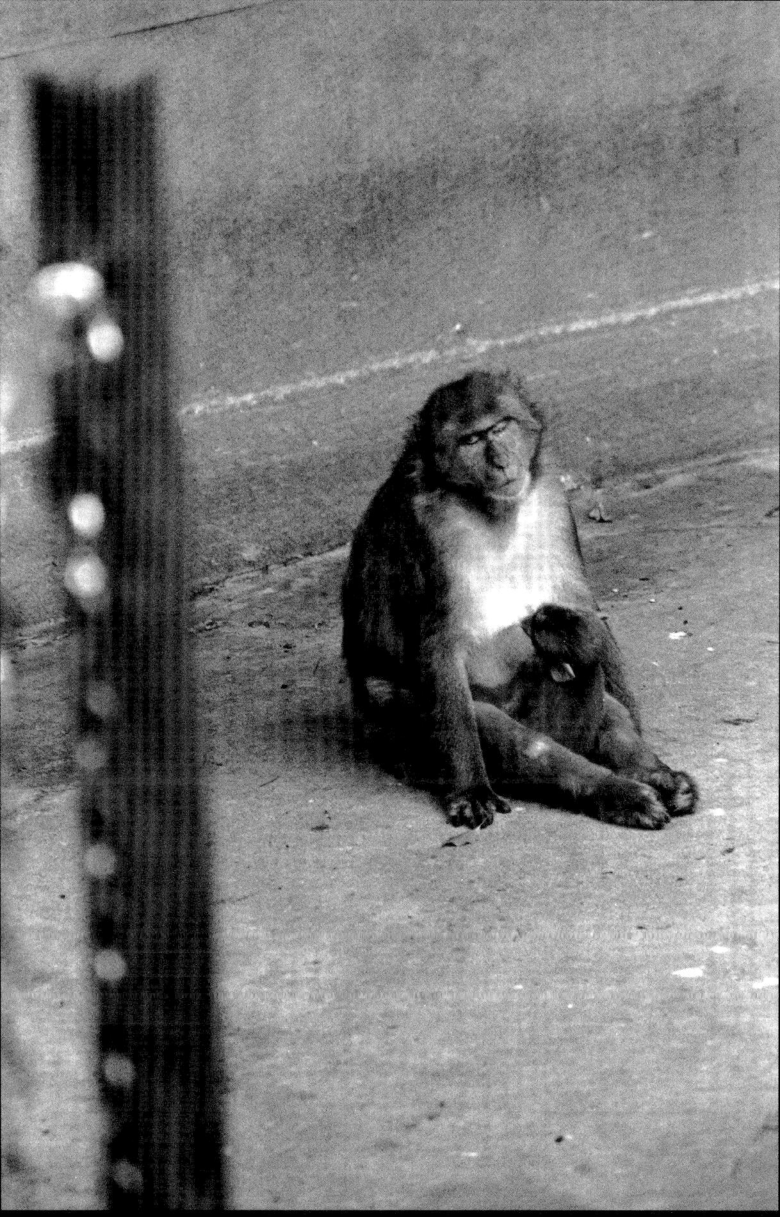

Ueno Zoo

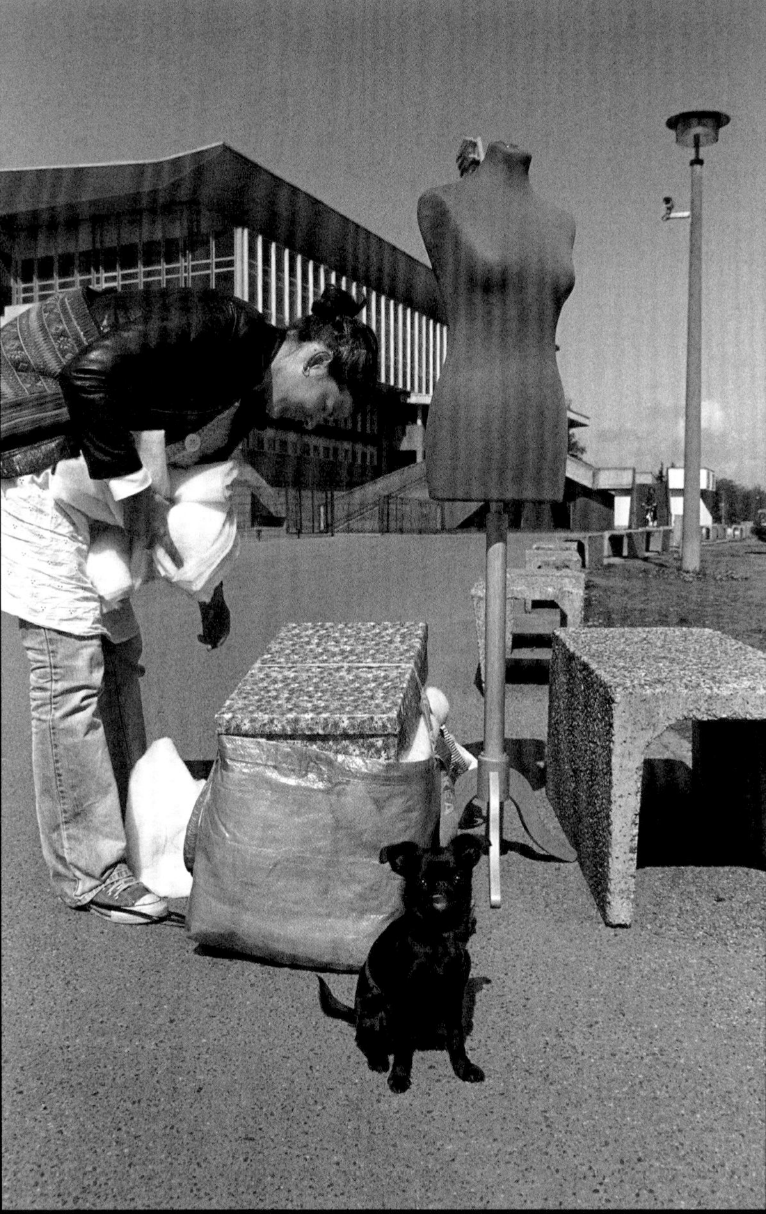

Friedrich-Ludwig-Jahn-Stadion, Max-Schmeling-Halle

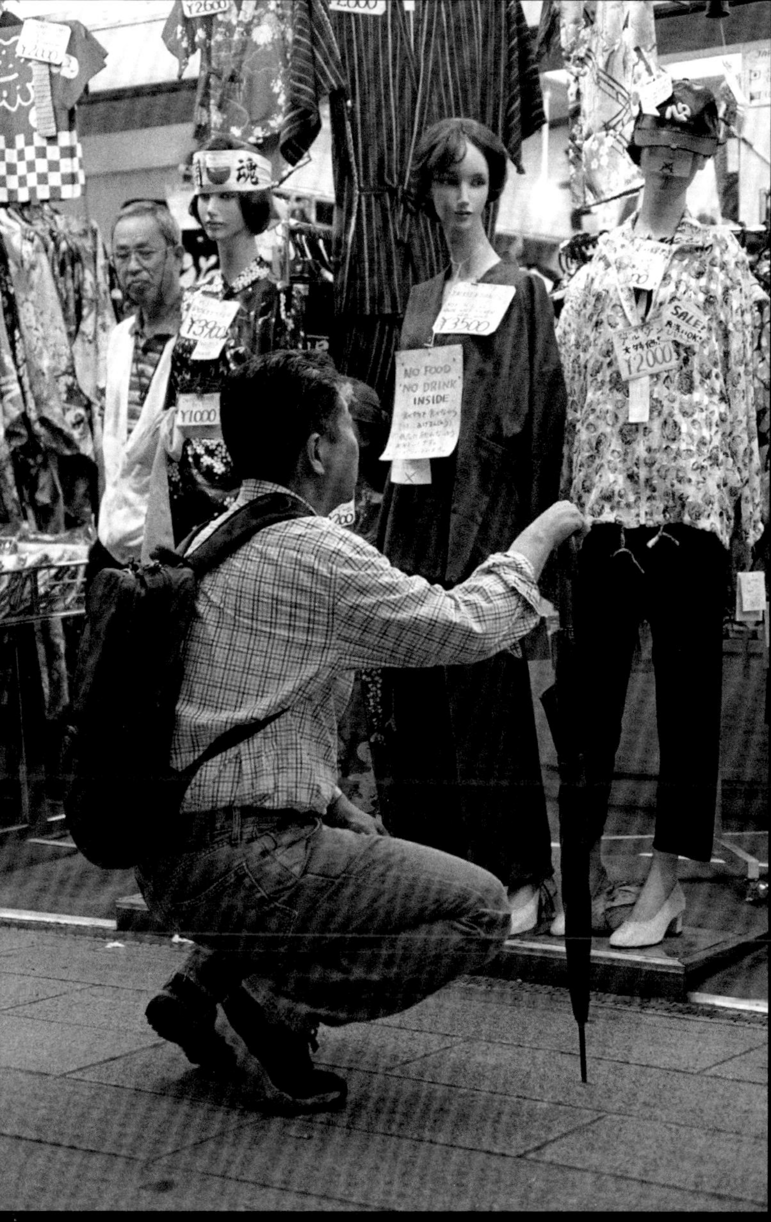

Asakusa

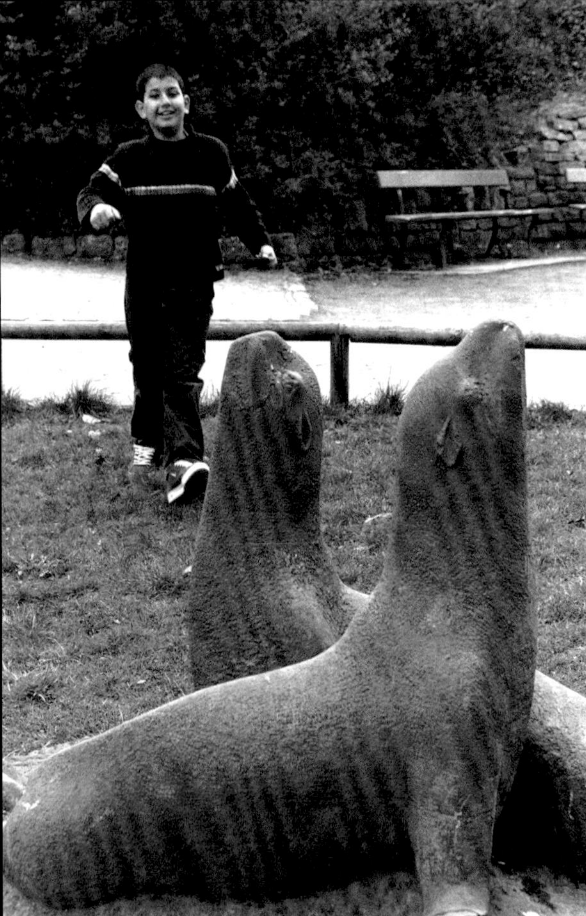
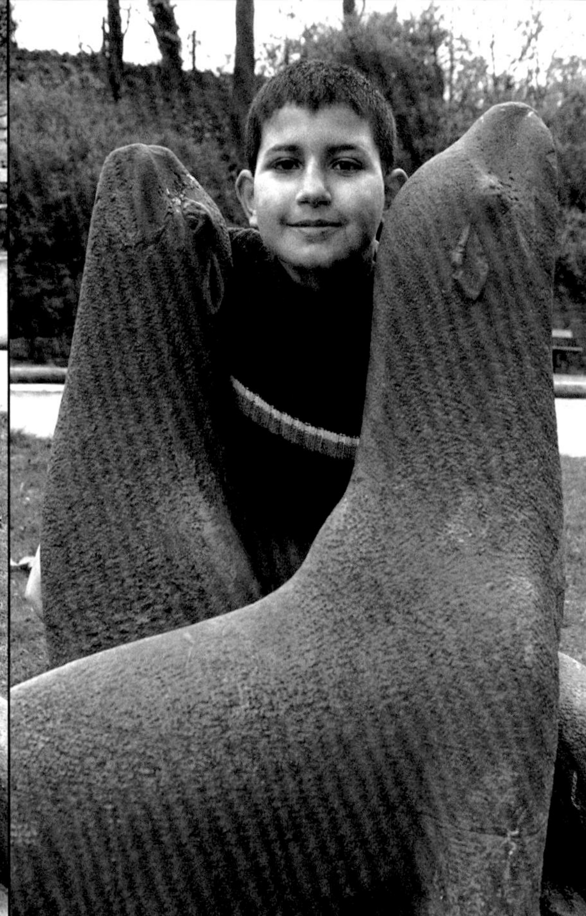

Charlottenburg

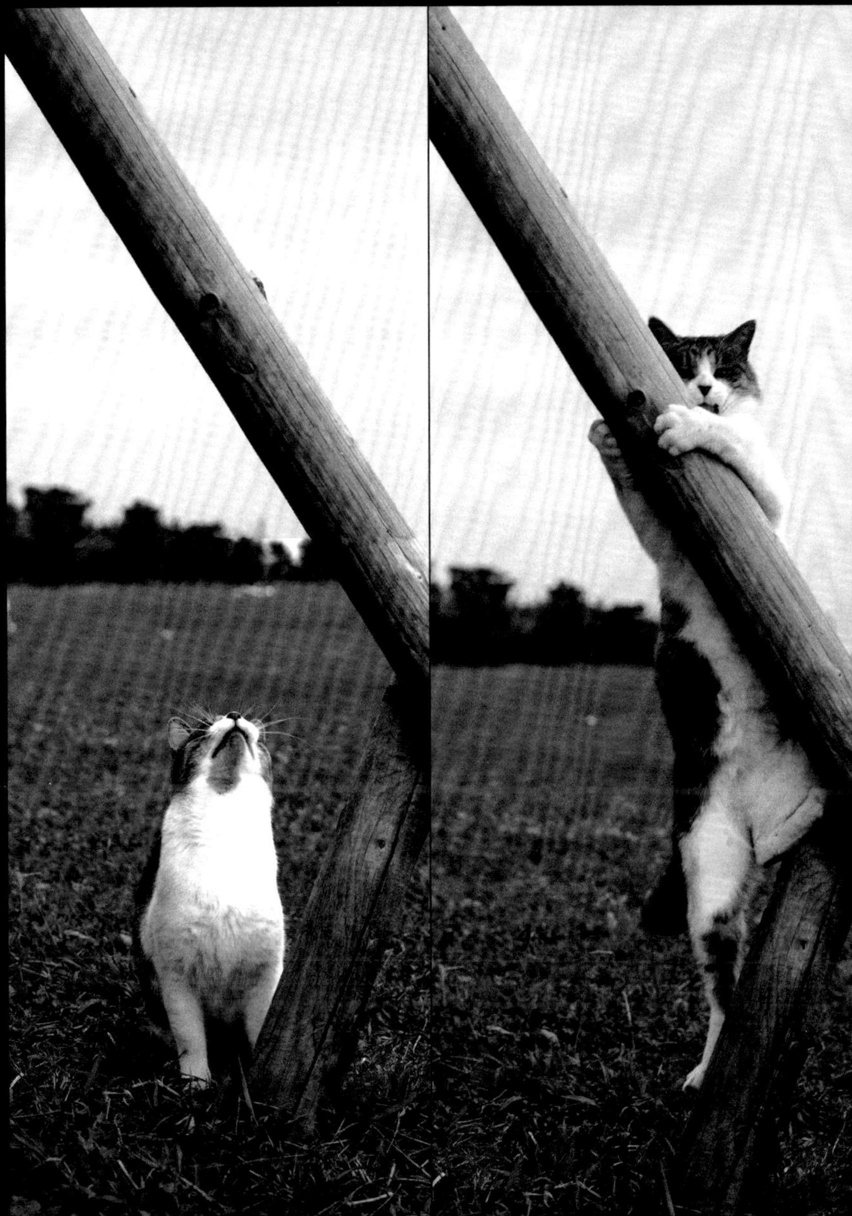

Kasai-Rinkai Park

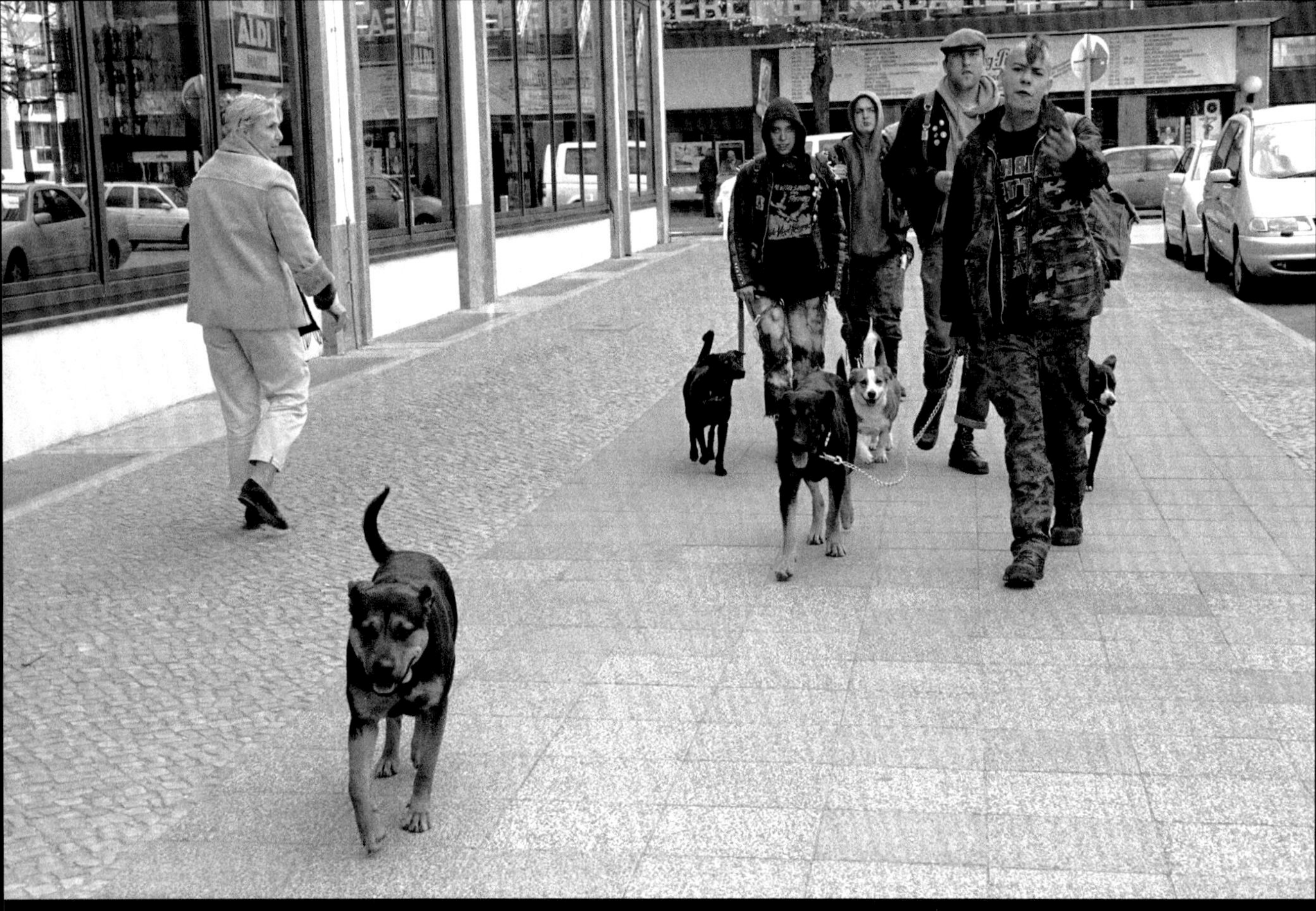

Theodor-Heuss-Platz

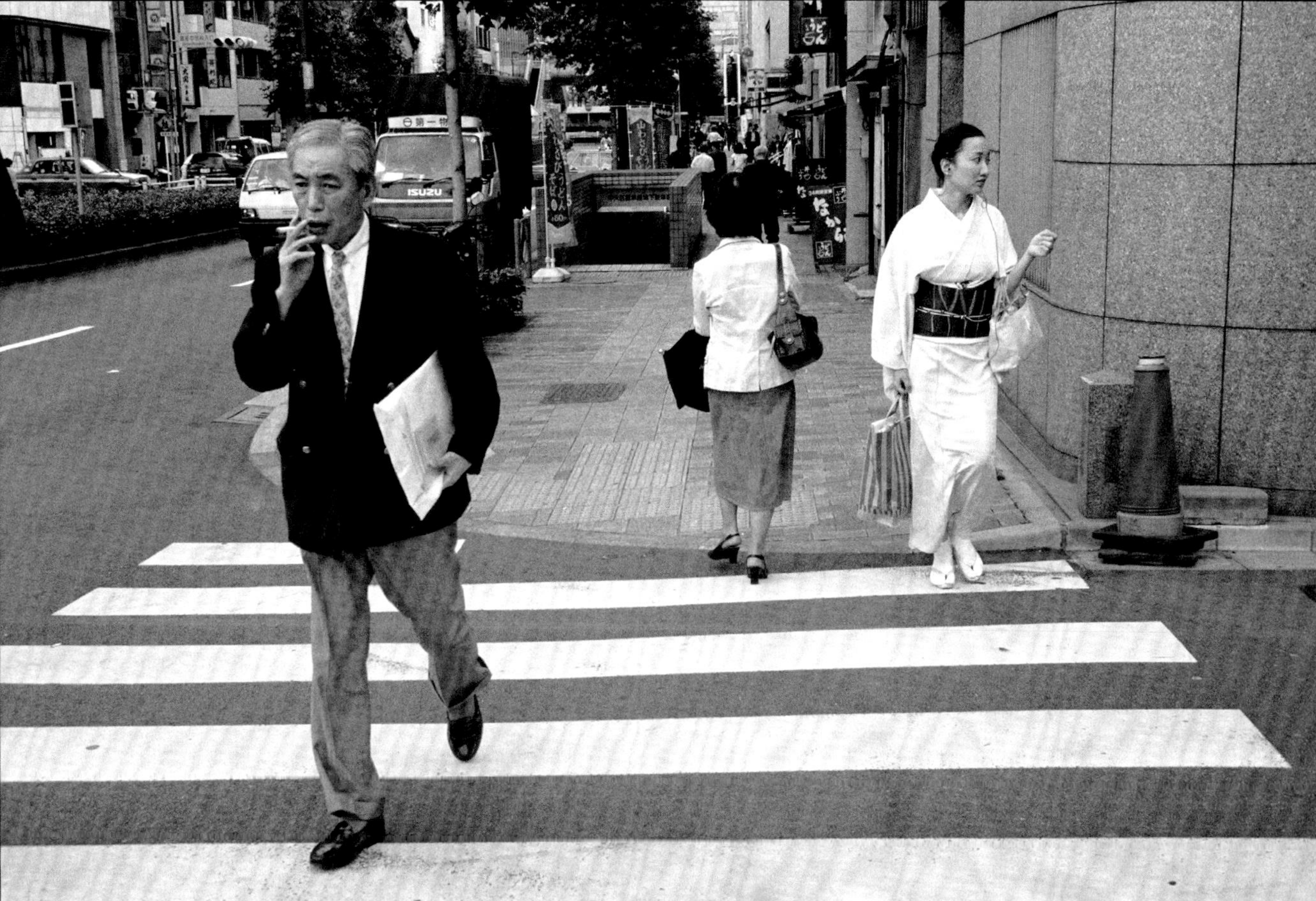

Tsukiji

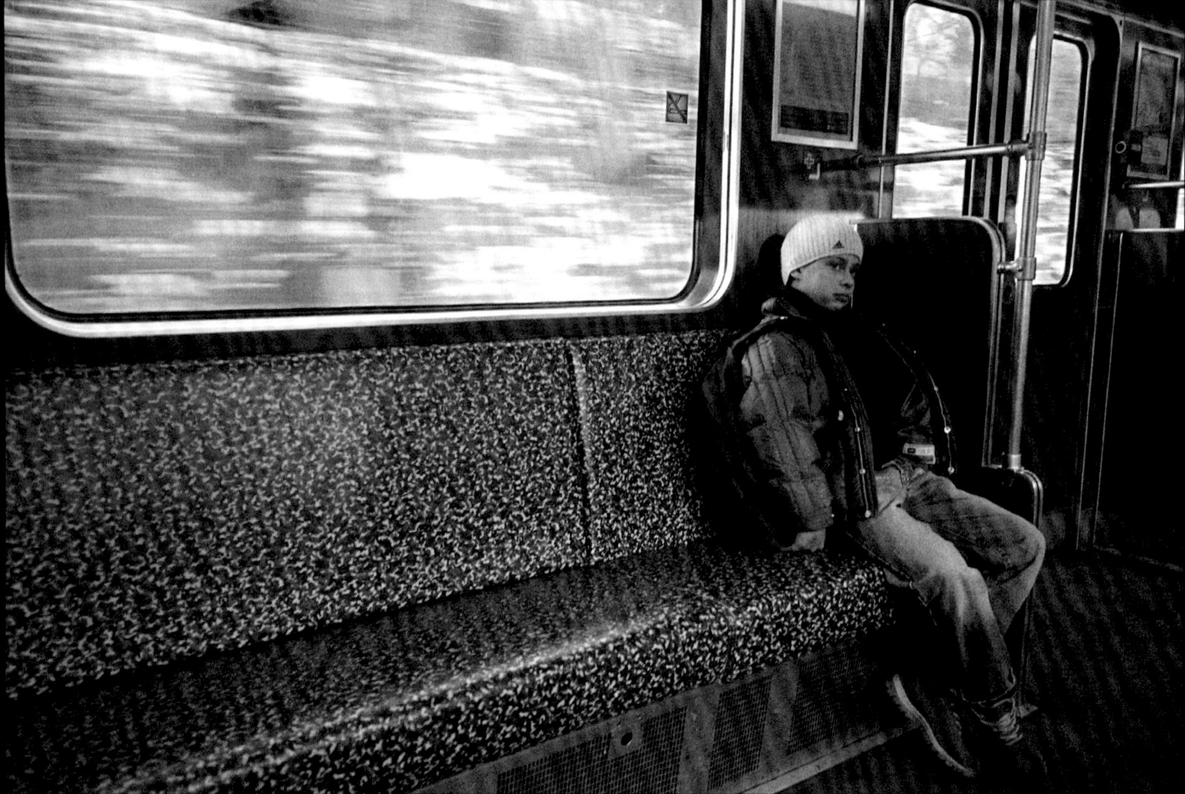

U-Bahn

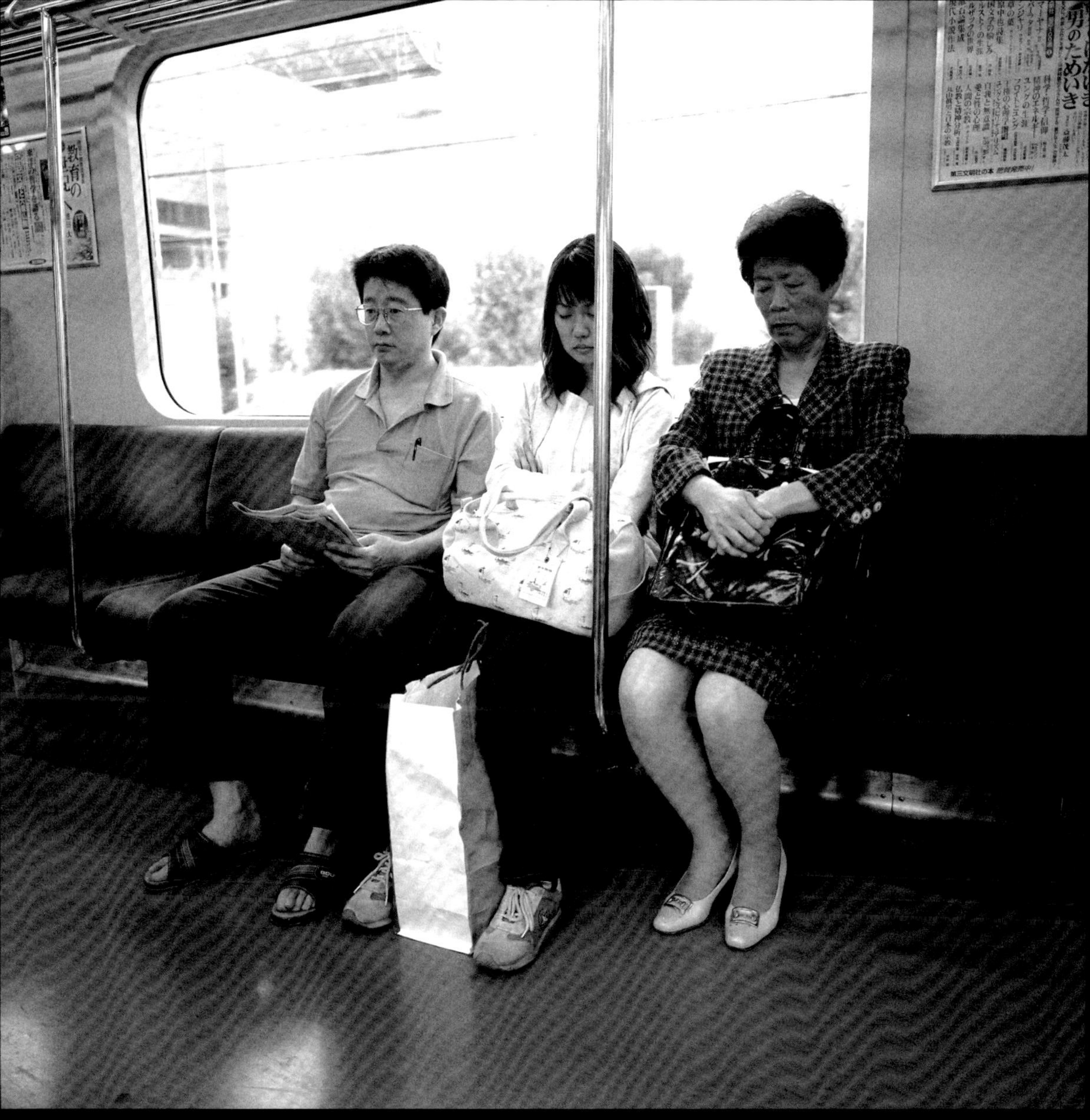

JR Line

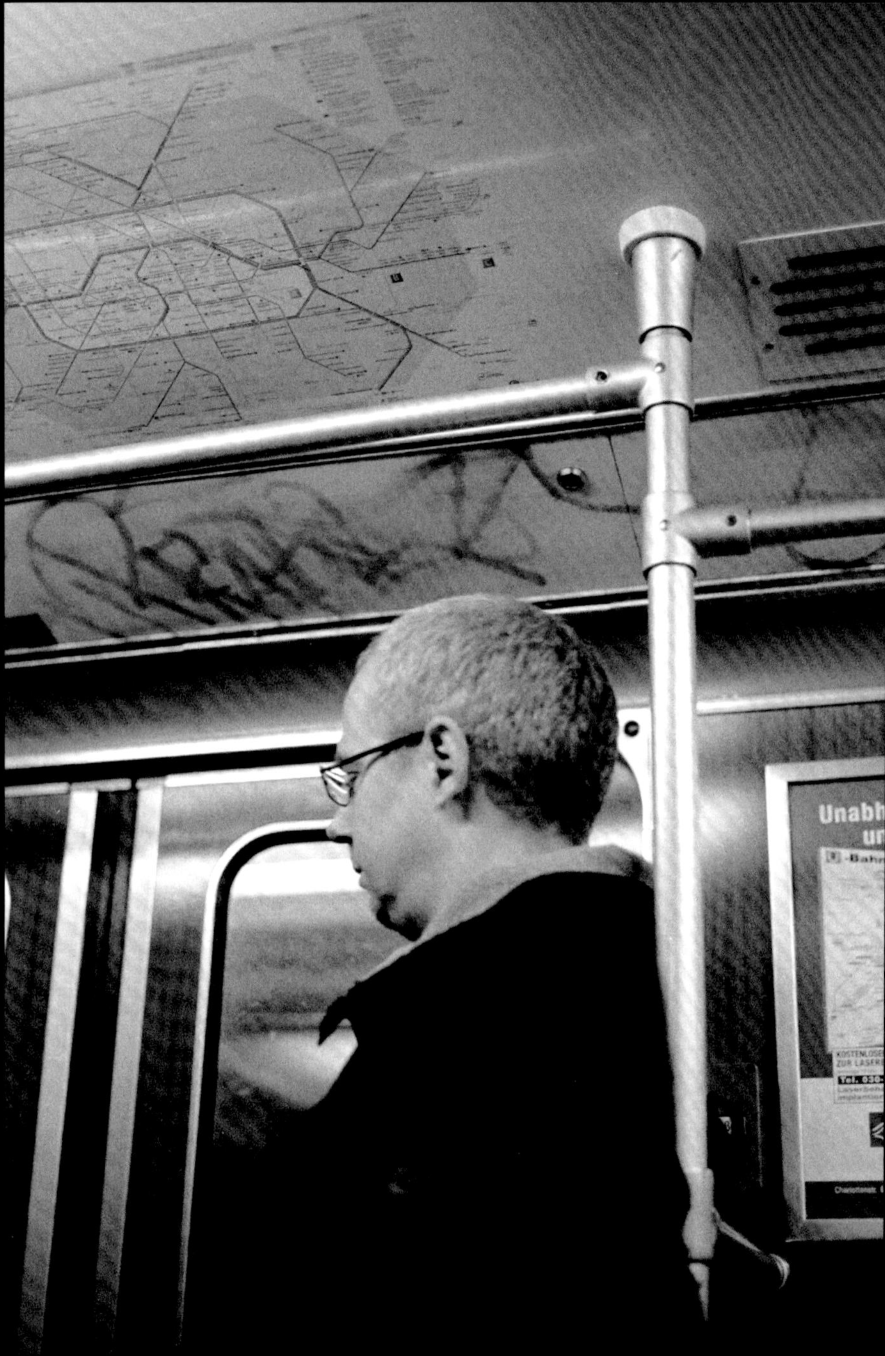

U-Bahn

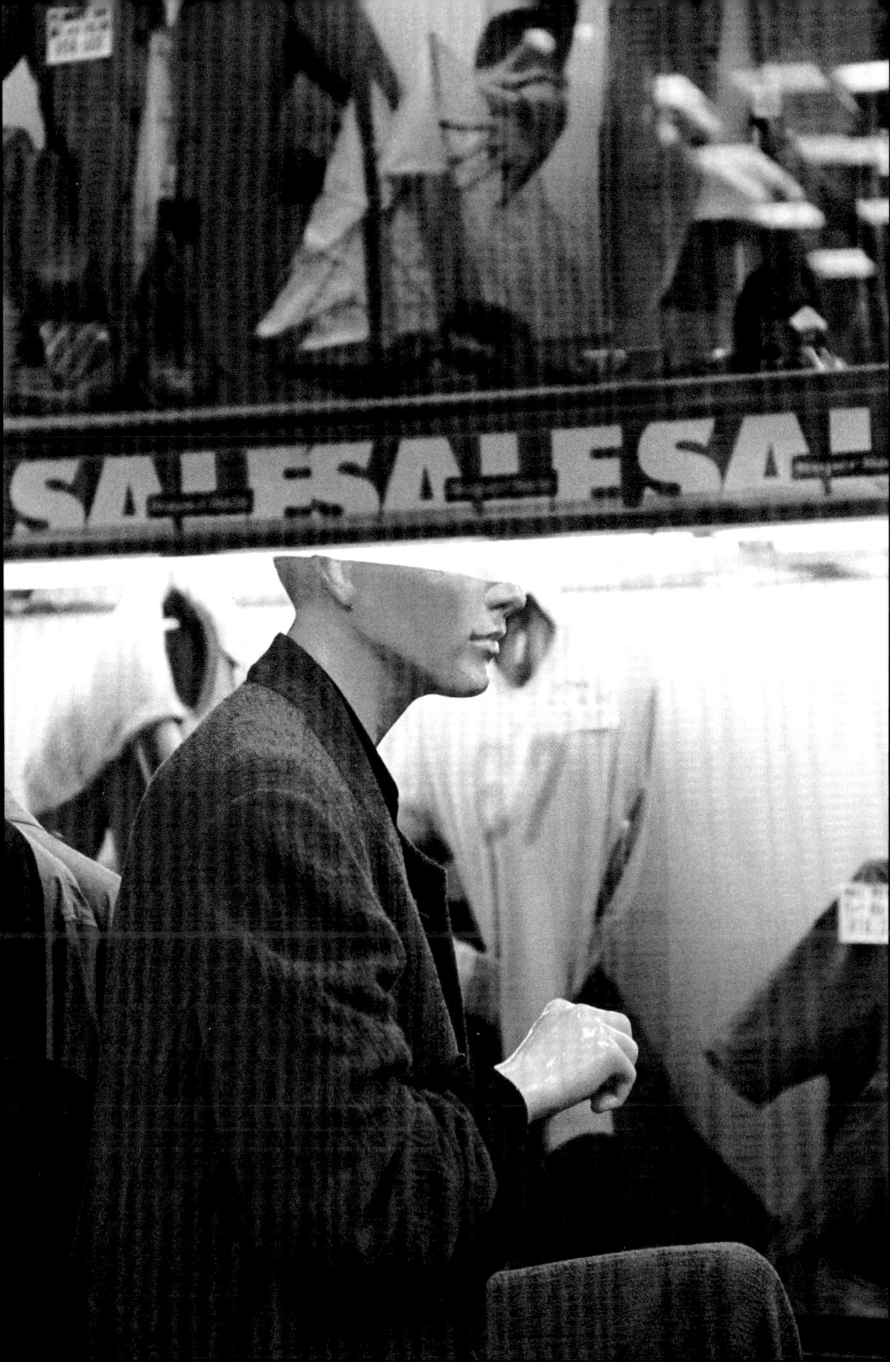

Asakusa

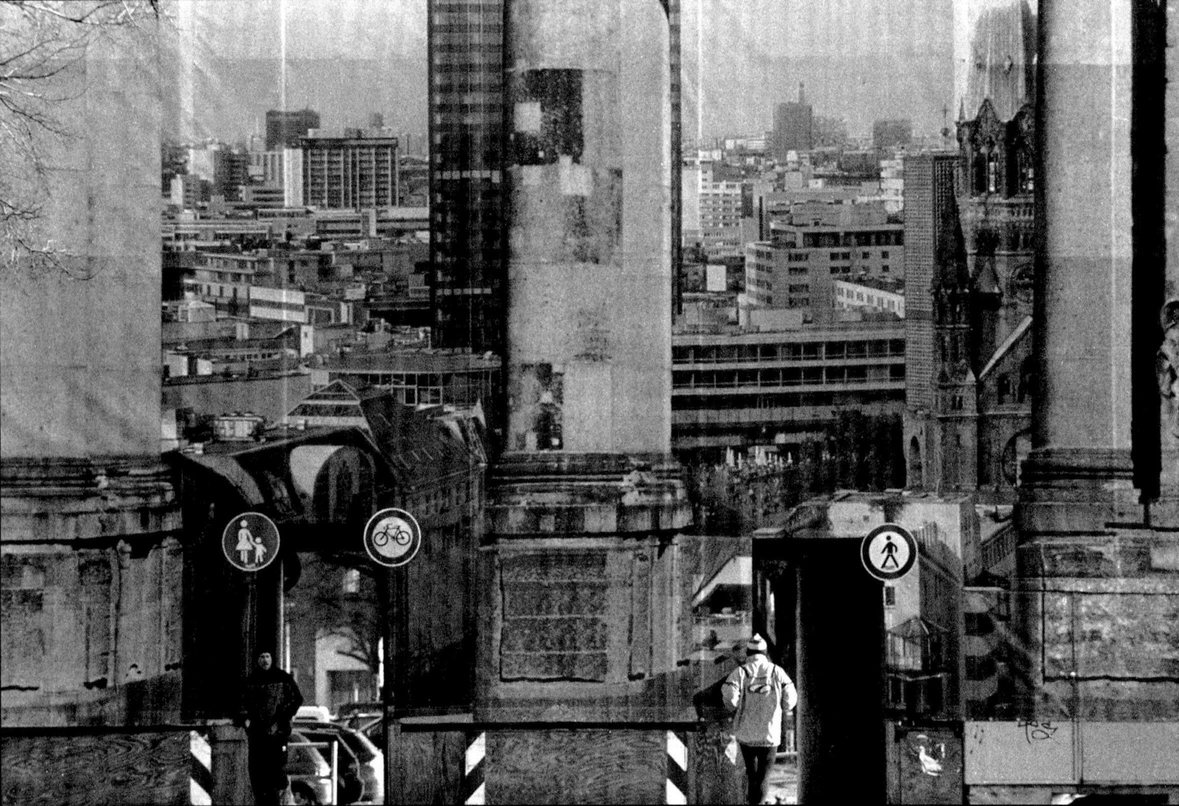

Straße des 17. Juni

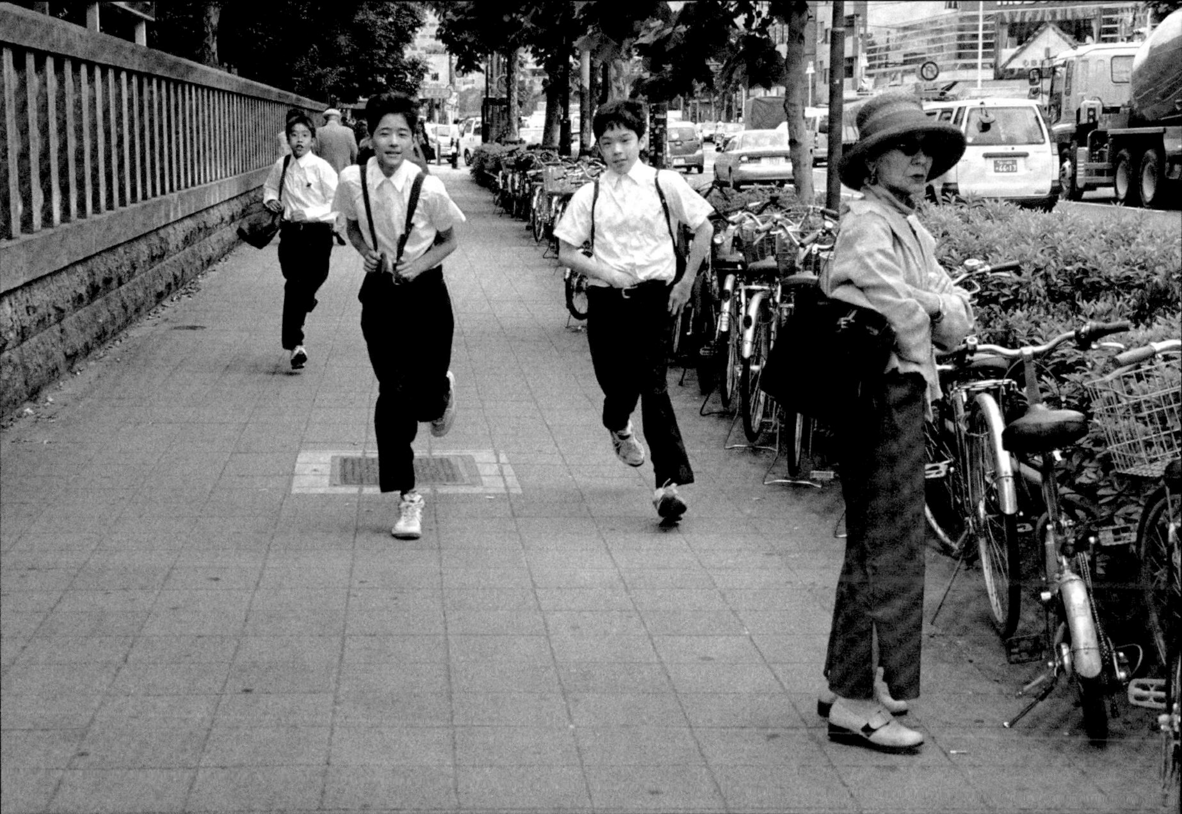

Tsukiji

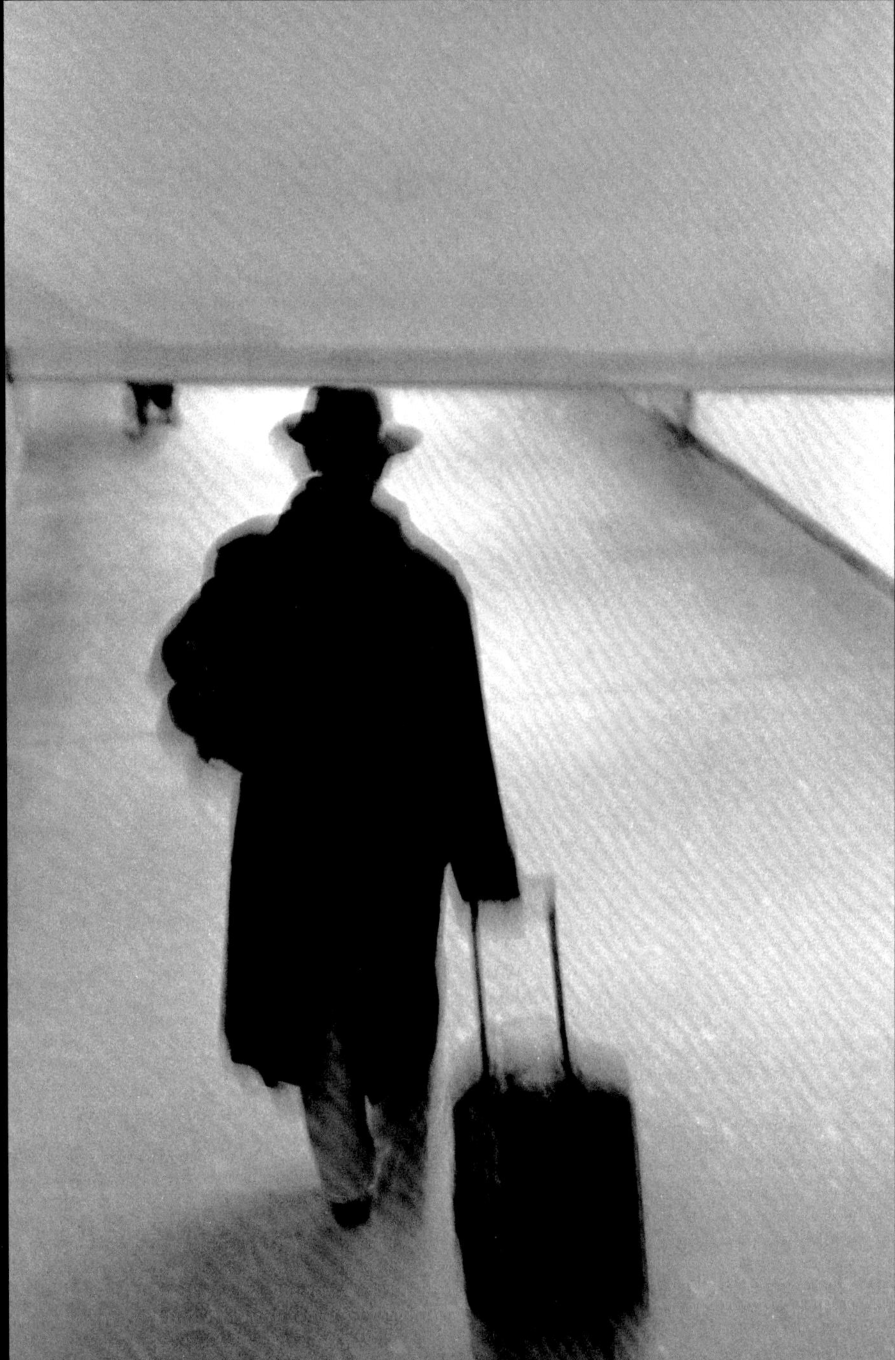

U-Bahnhof Zoologischer Garten

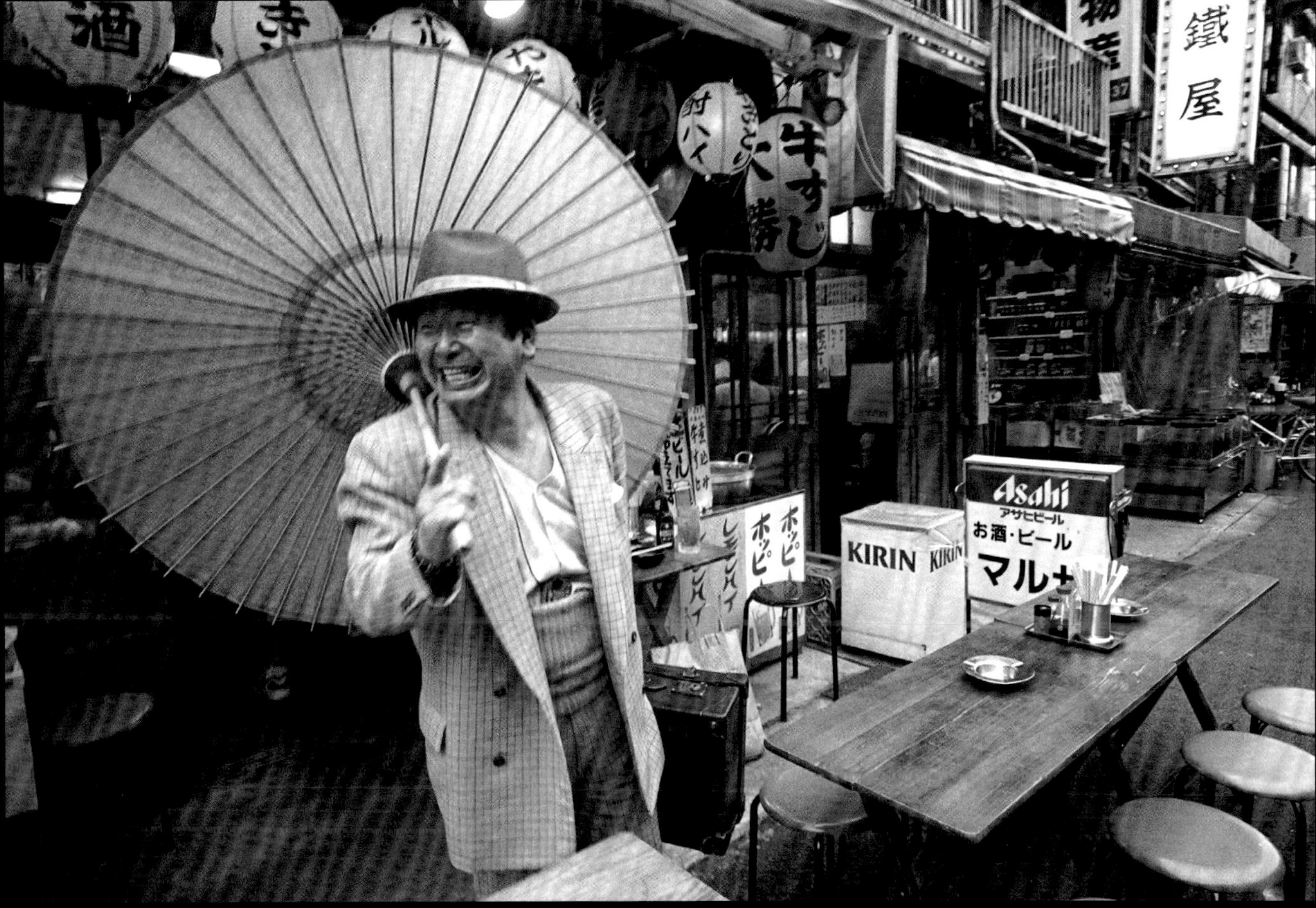

Asakusa

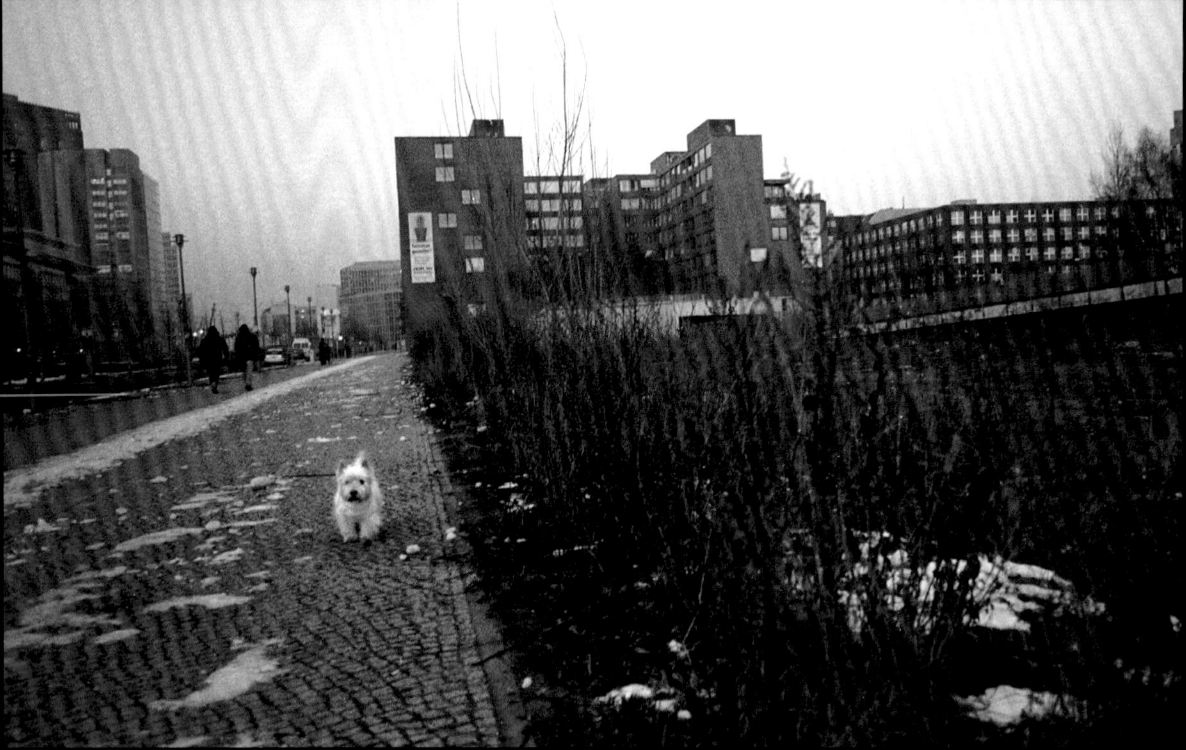

Mendelssohn-Bartholdy-Park

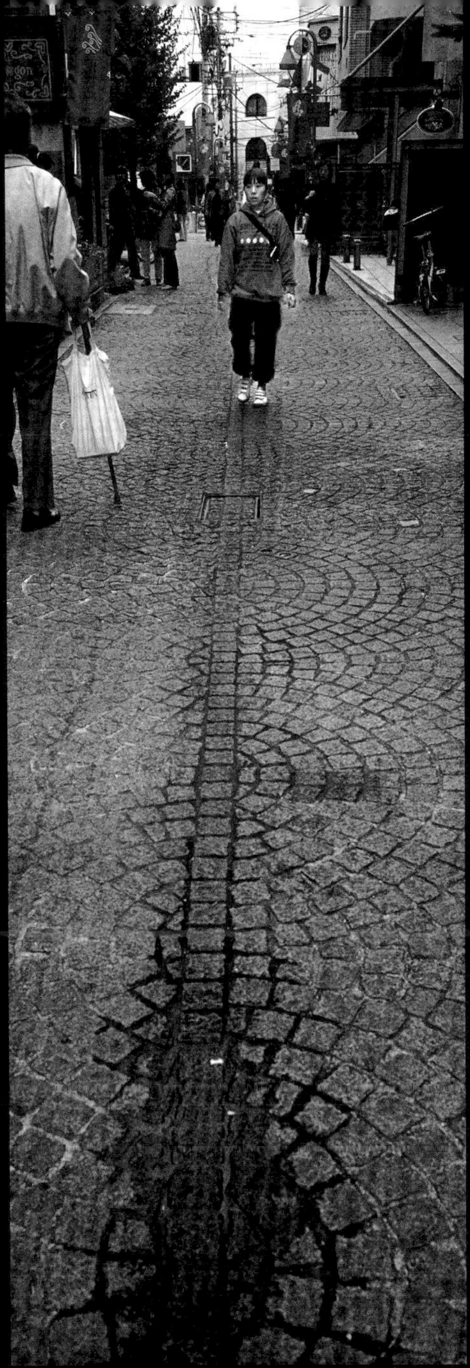

Jiyugaoka

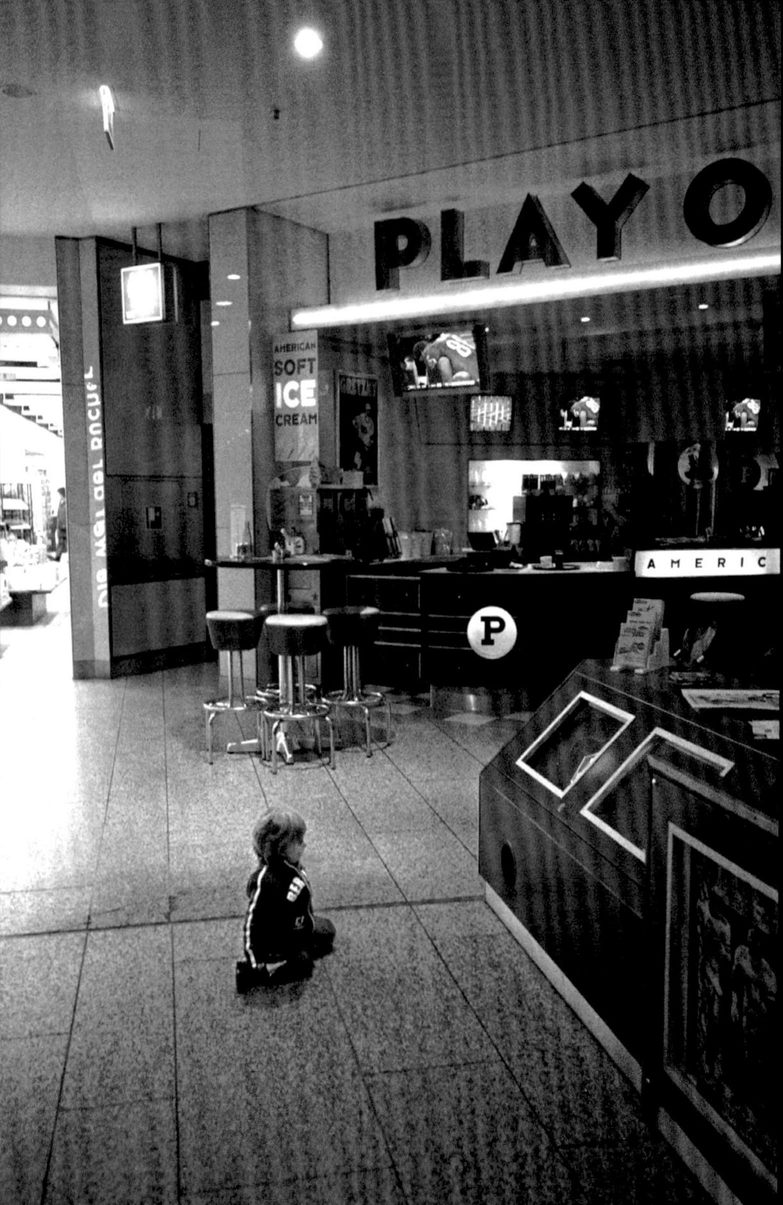

Potsdamer Platz Arkaden

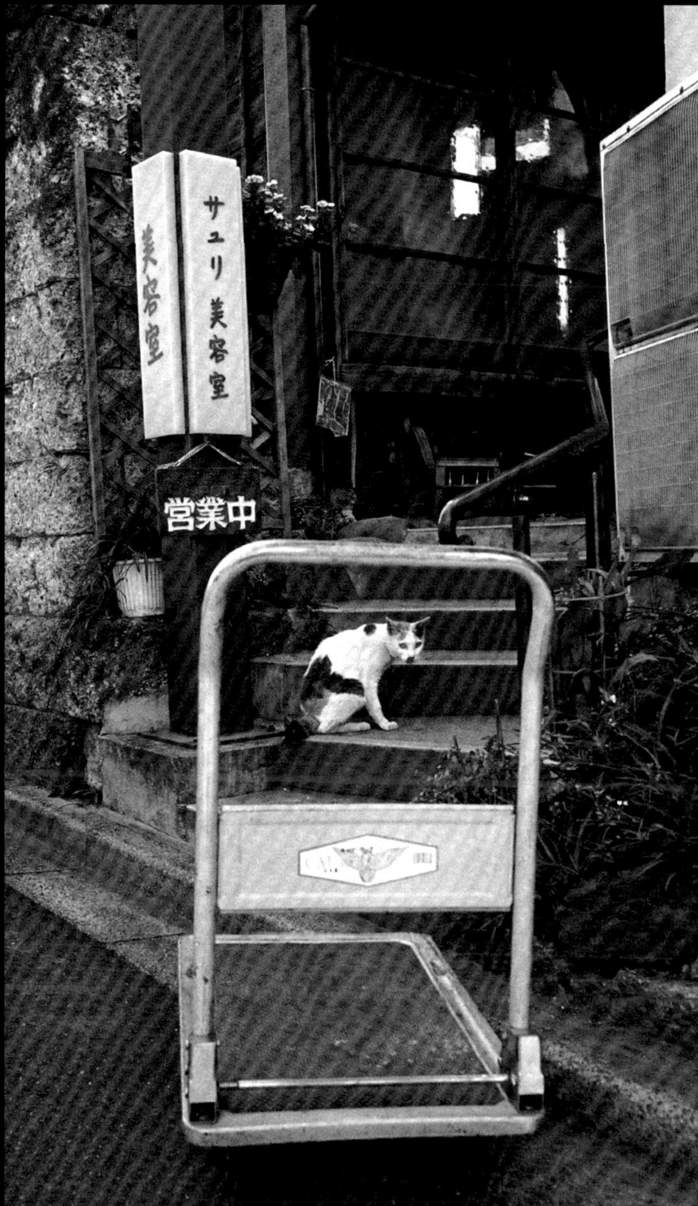

Yanaka

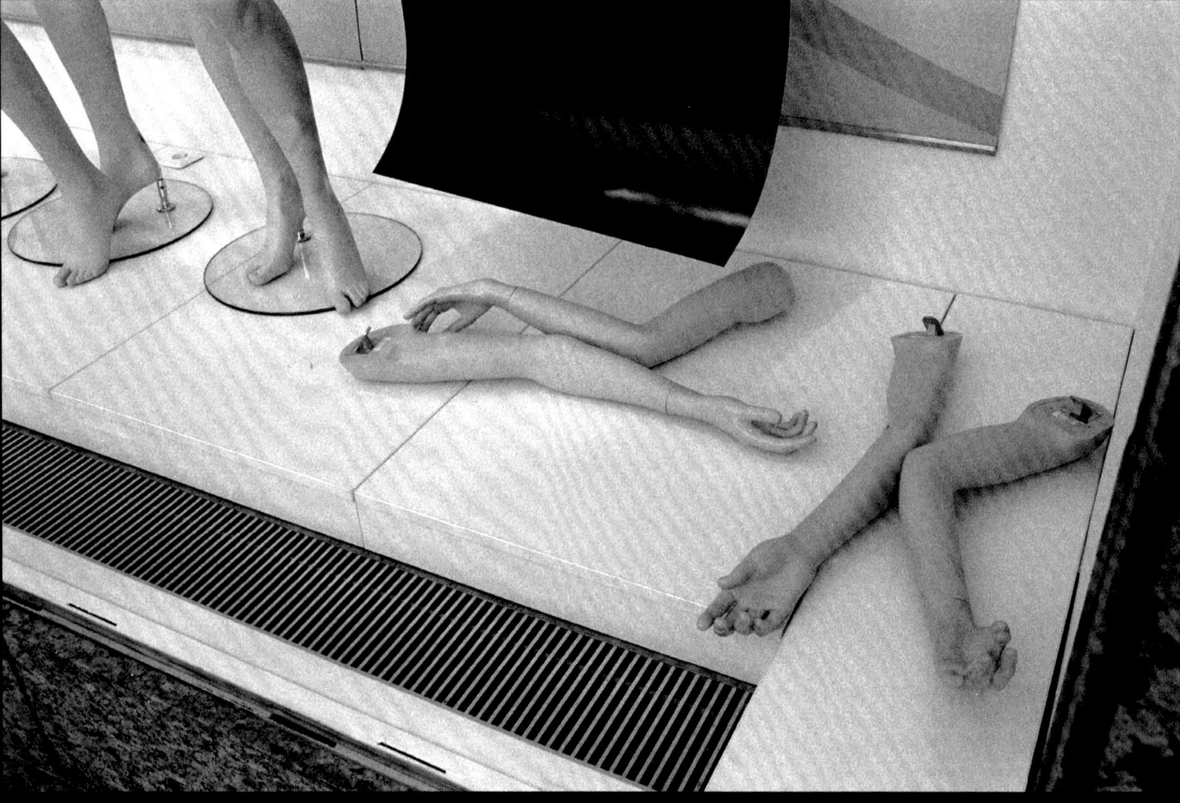

Wilmersdorfer Straße

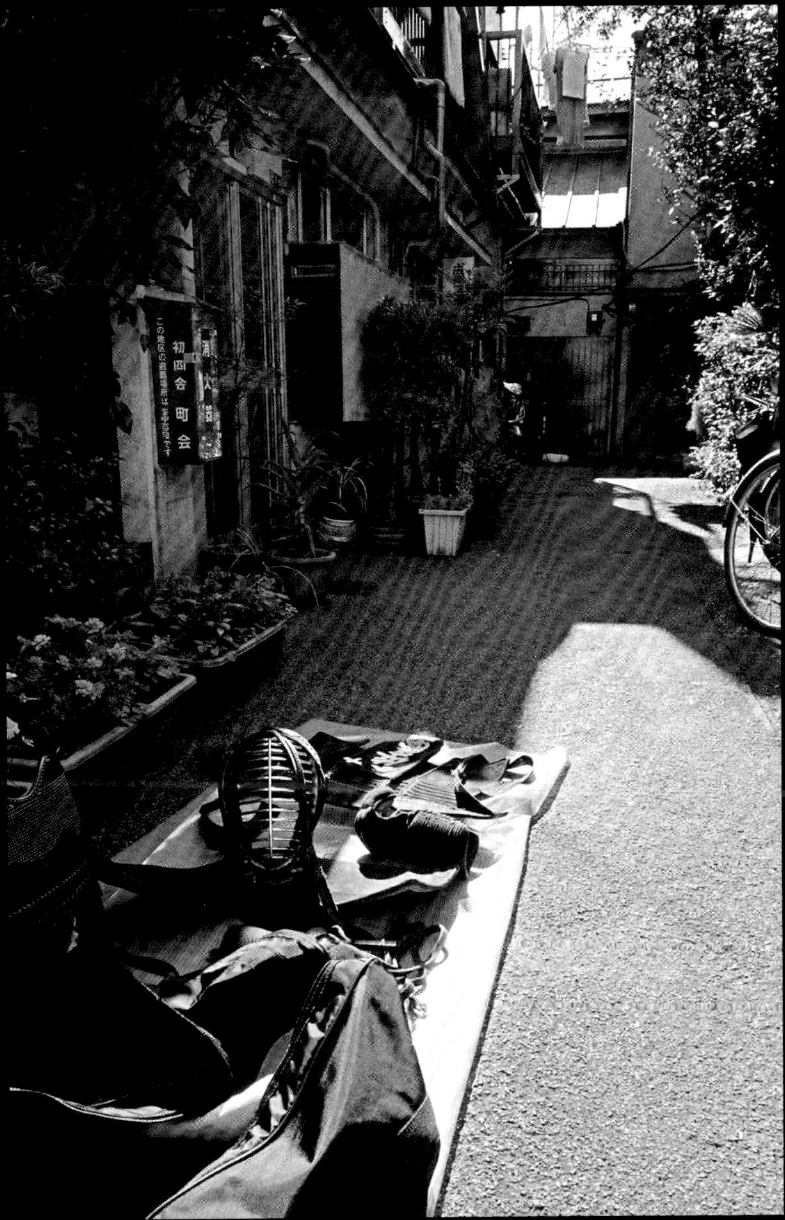

Yanaka

三四

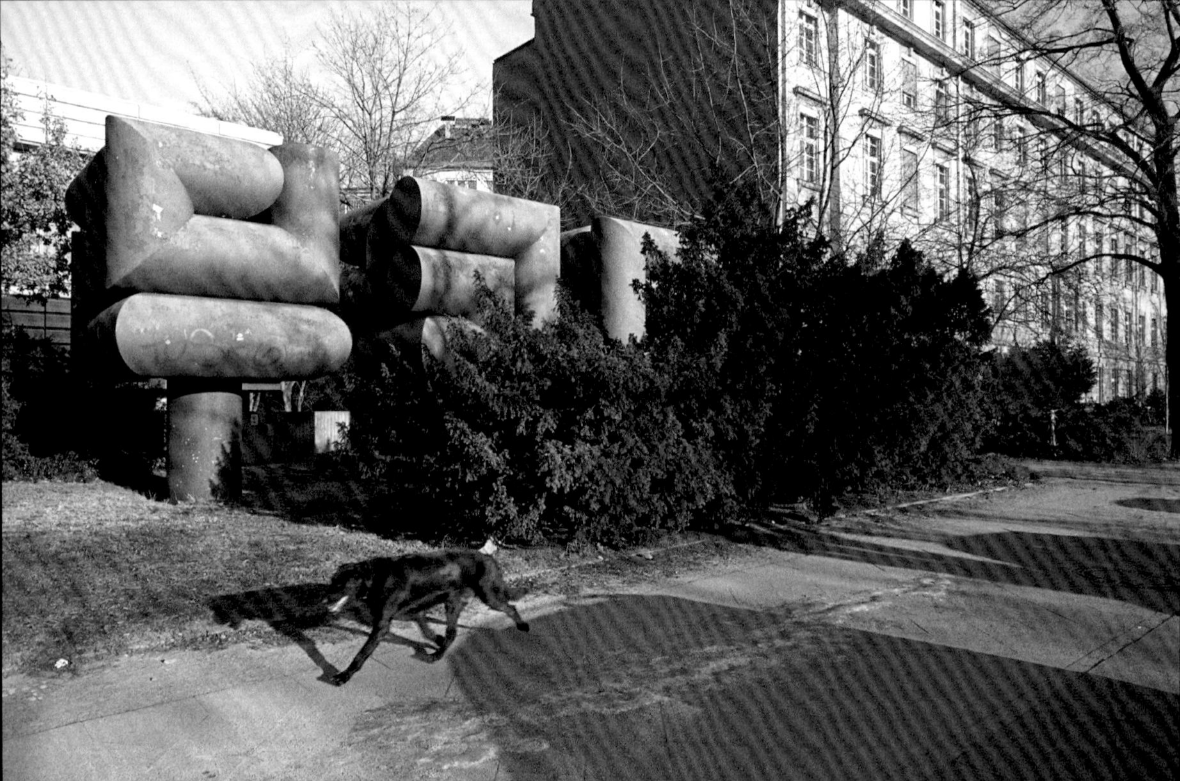

Straße des 17. Juni

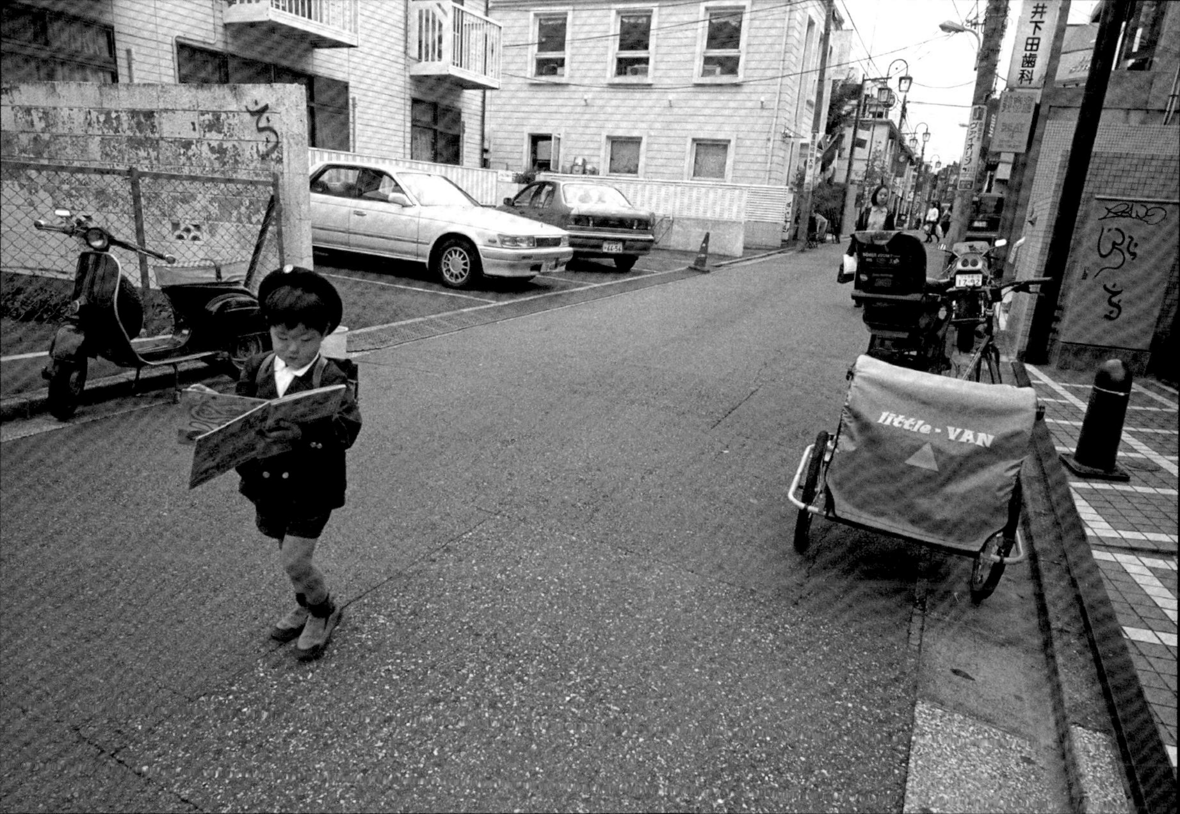

Jiyugaoka

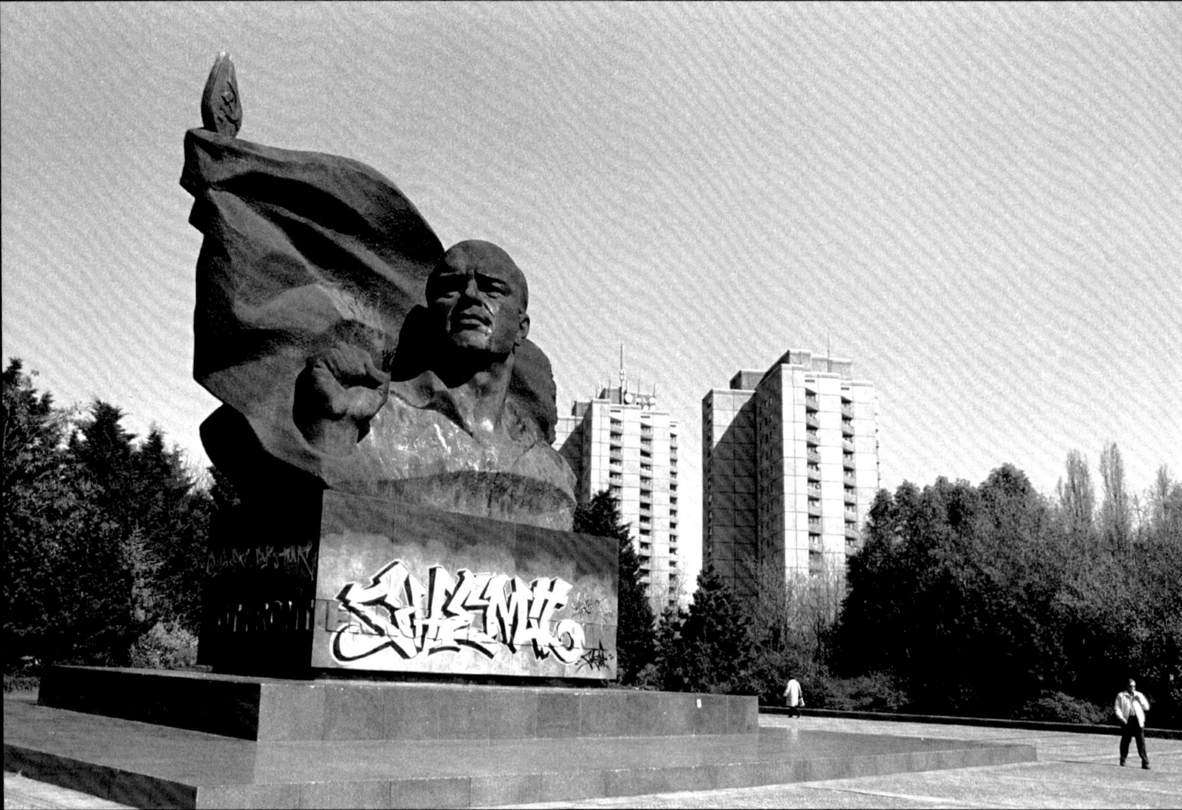

Greifswalder Straße

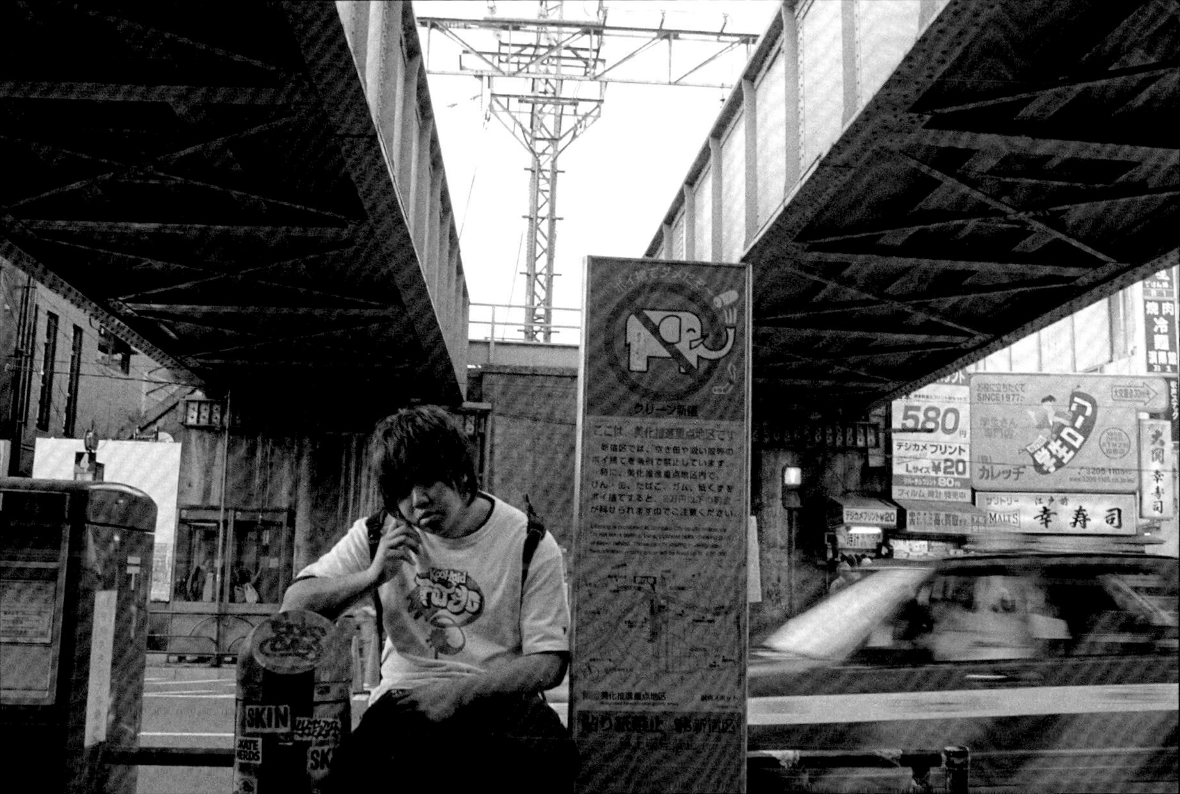

Takadanobaba

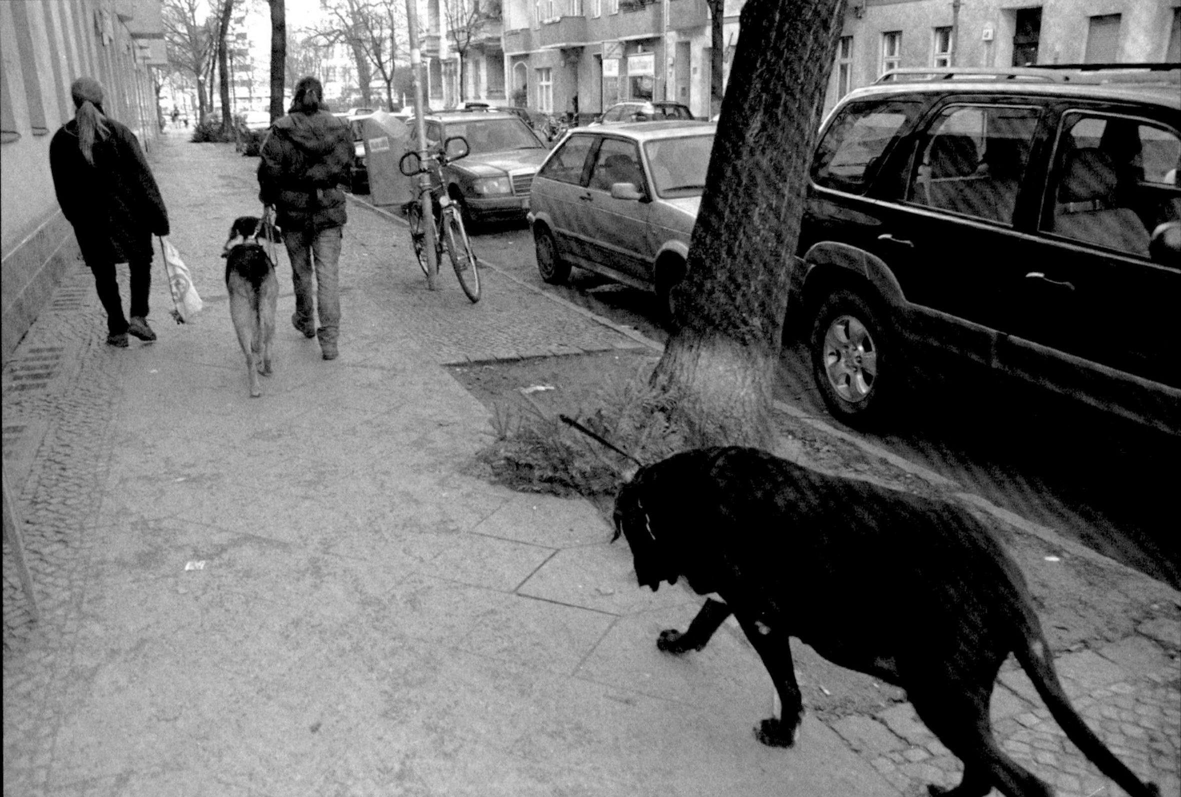

Neukölln

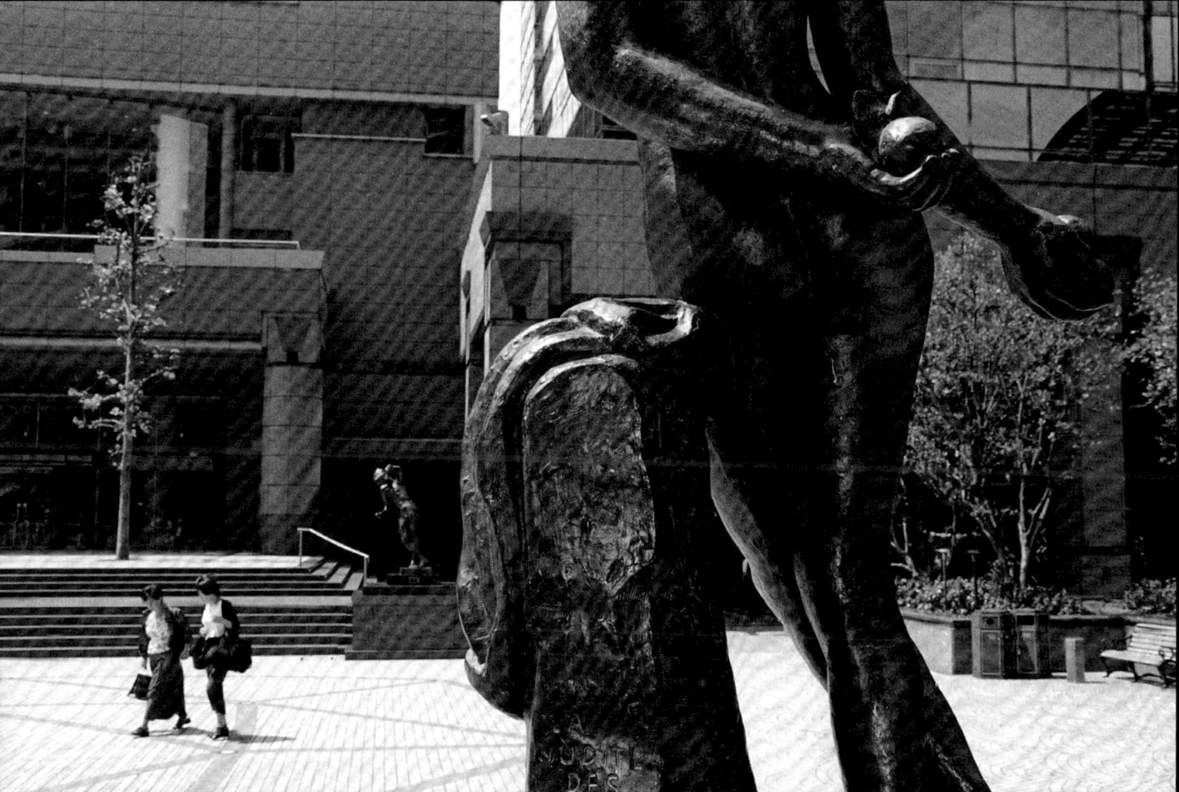

Ebisu-Garden Place

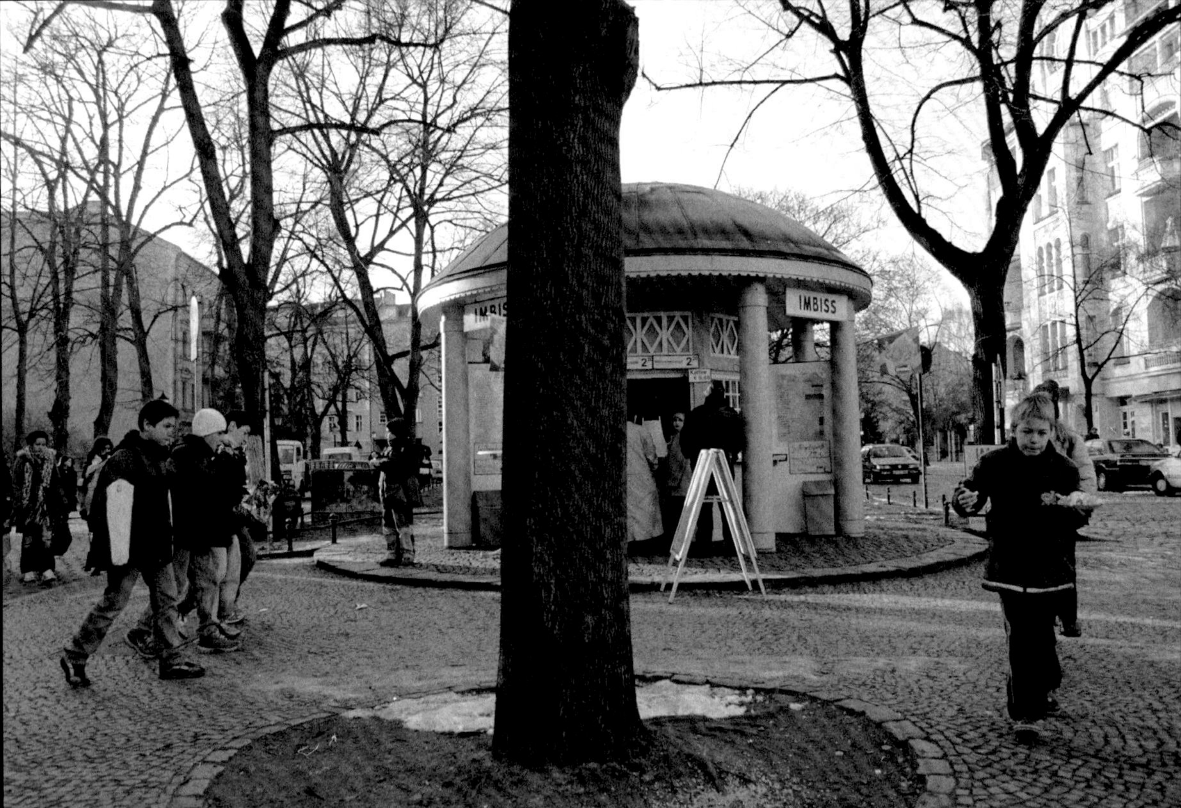

Neukölln

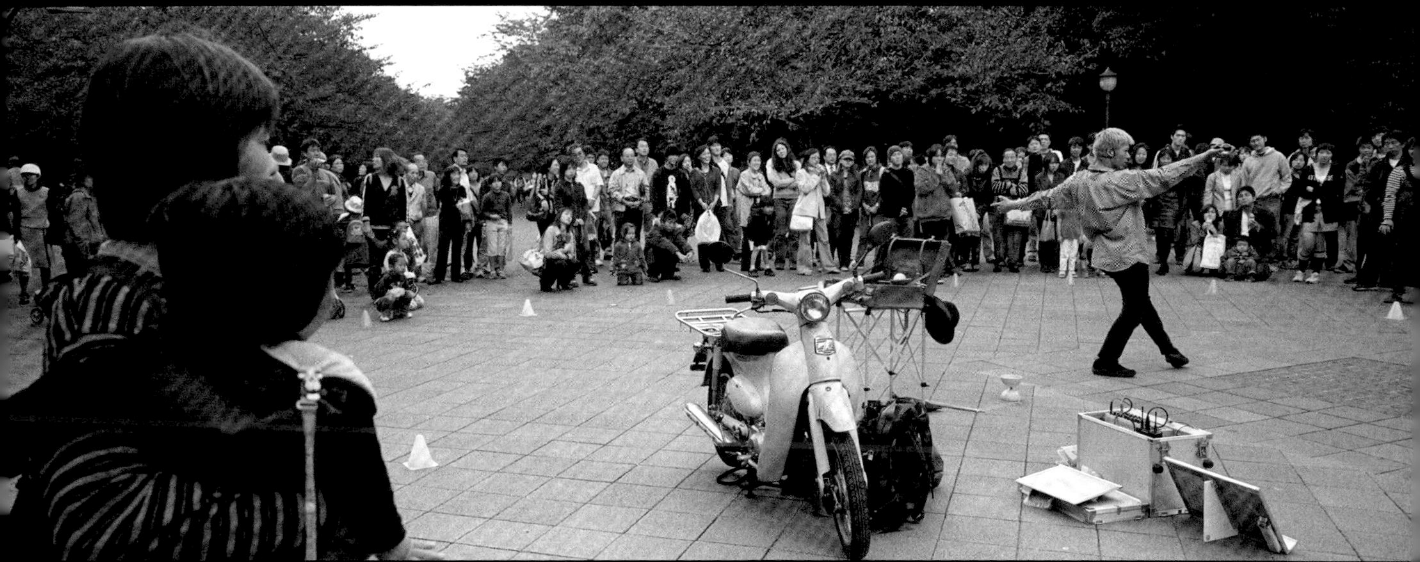

Ueno Park

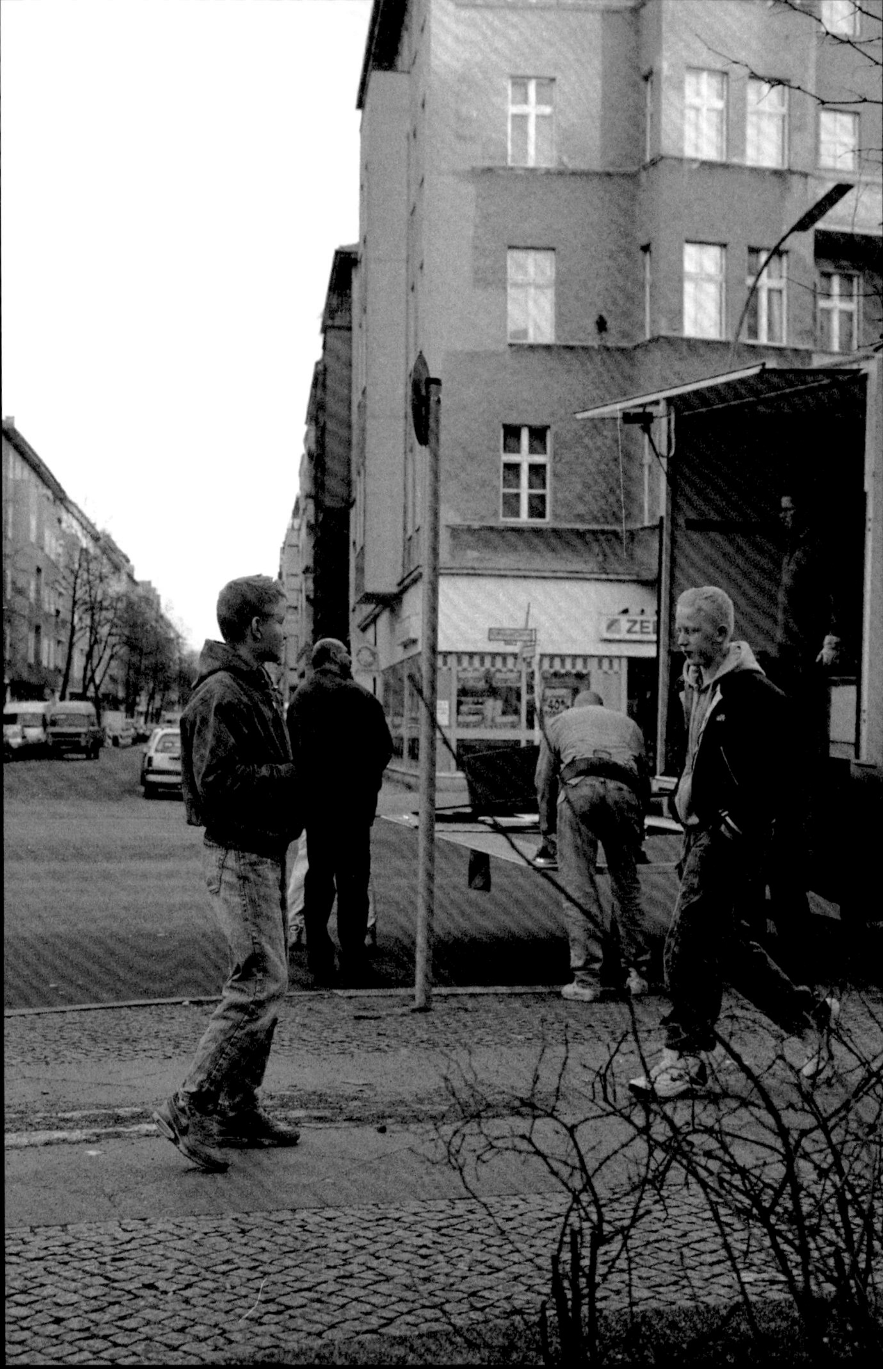

Kreuzberg

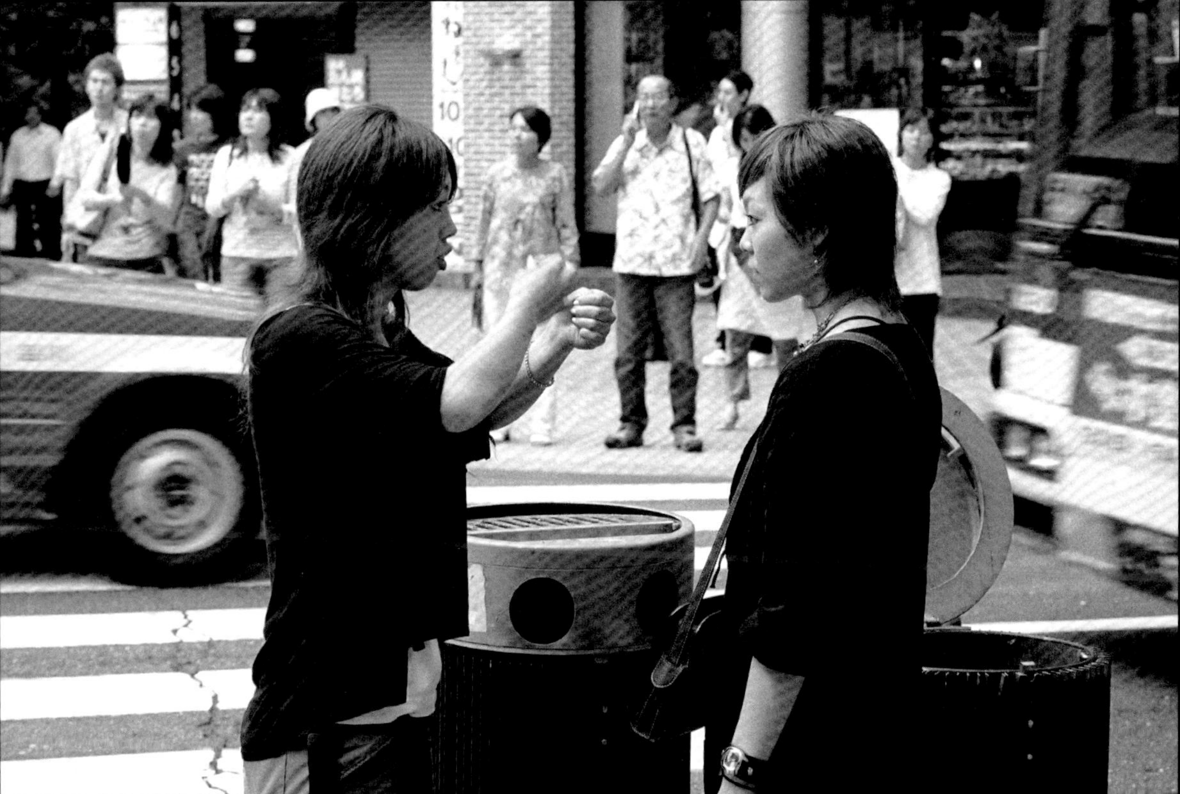

Shibuya

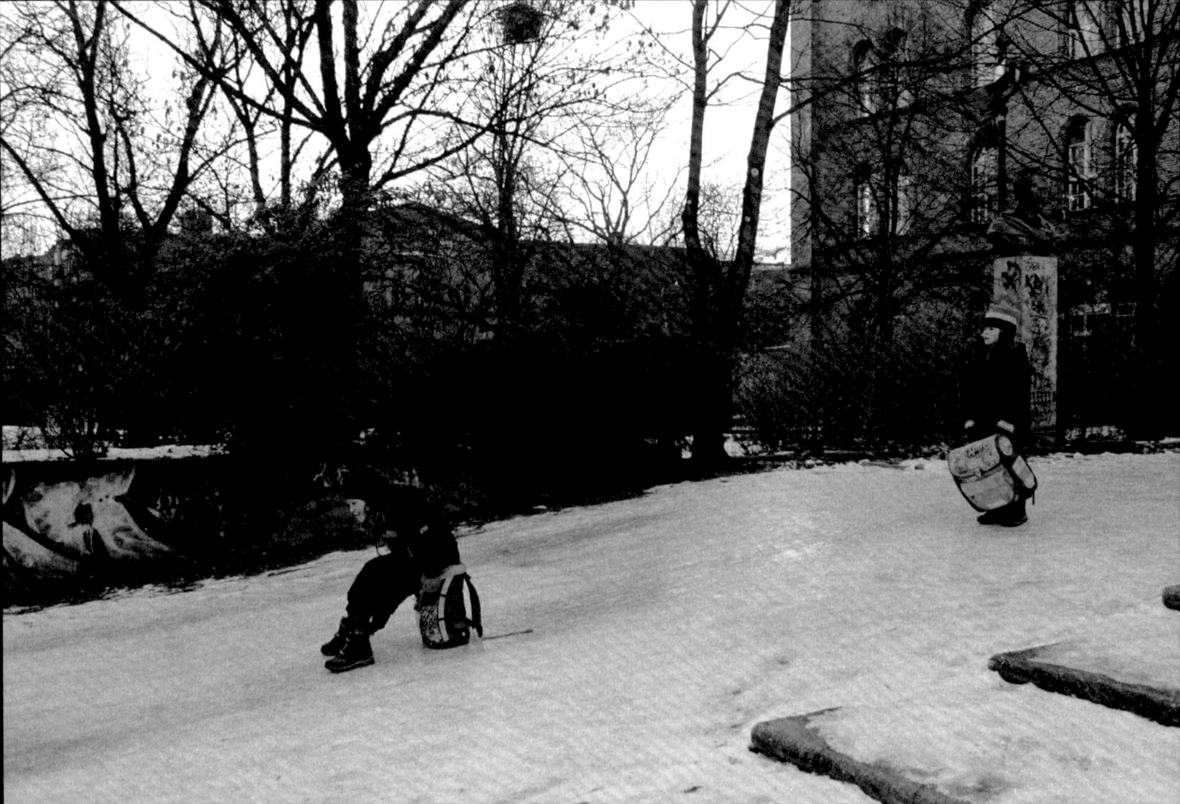

Kreuzberg

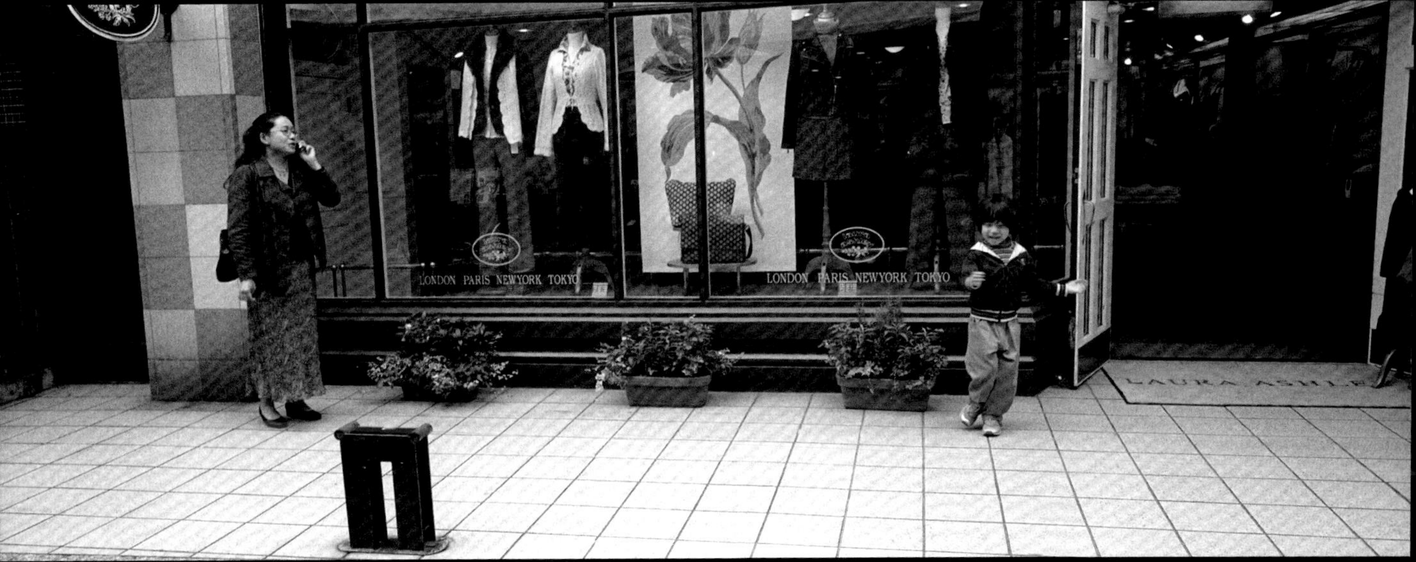

Jiyugaoka

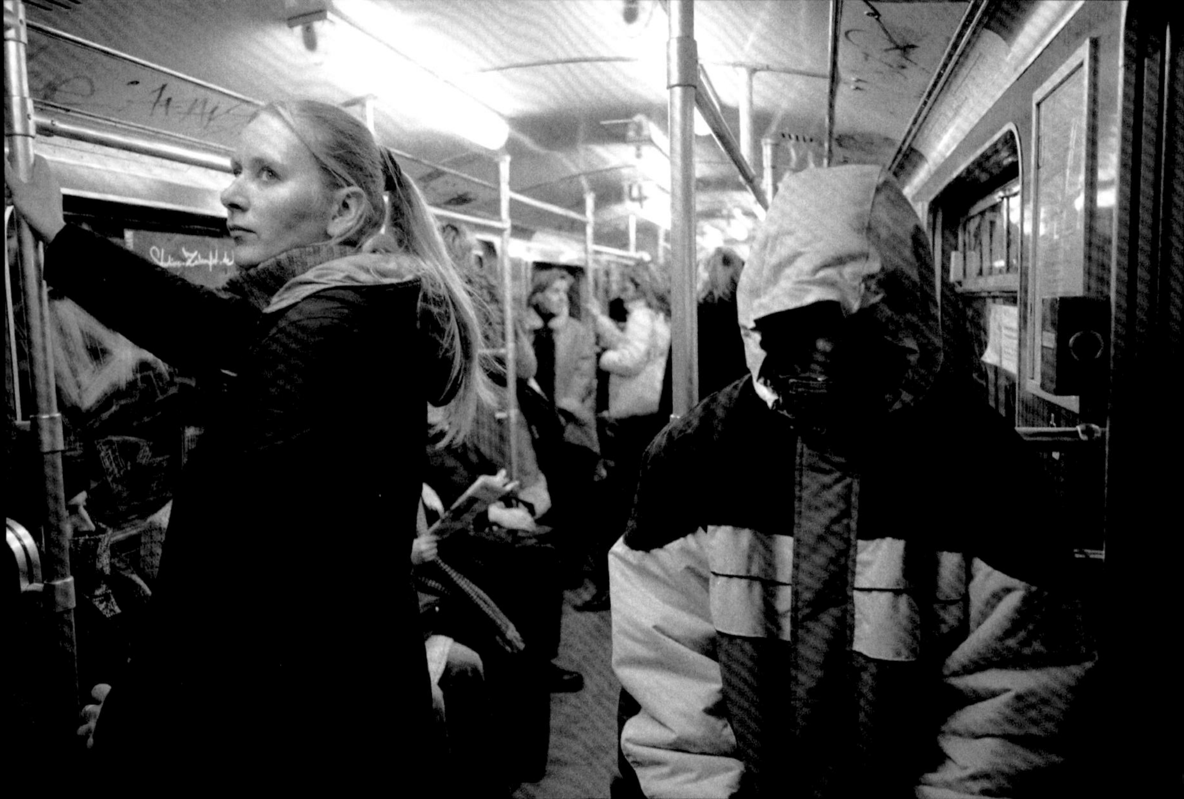

U-Bahn

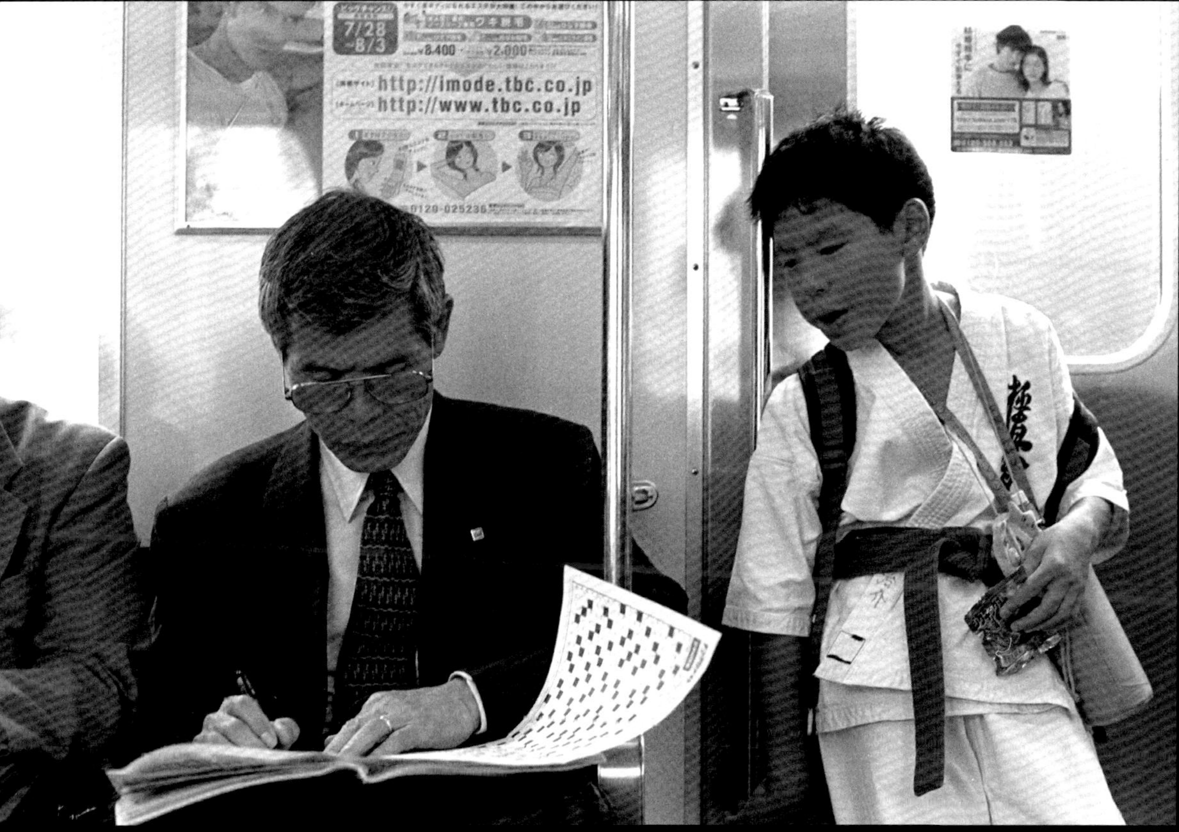
7/28
~8/3
¥8,400
¥2,000
http://imode.tbc.co.jp
http://www.tbc.co.jp
0120-025236

JR Line

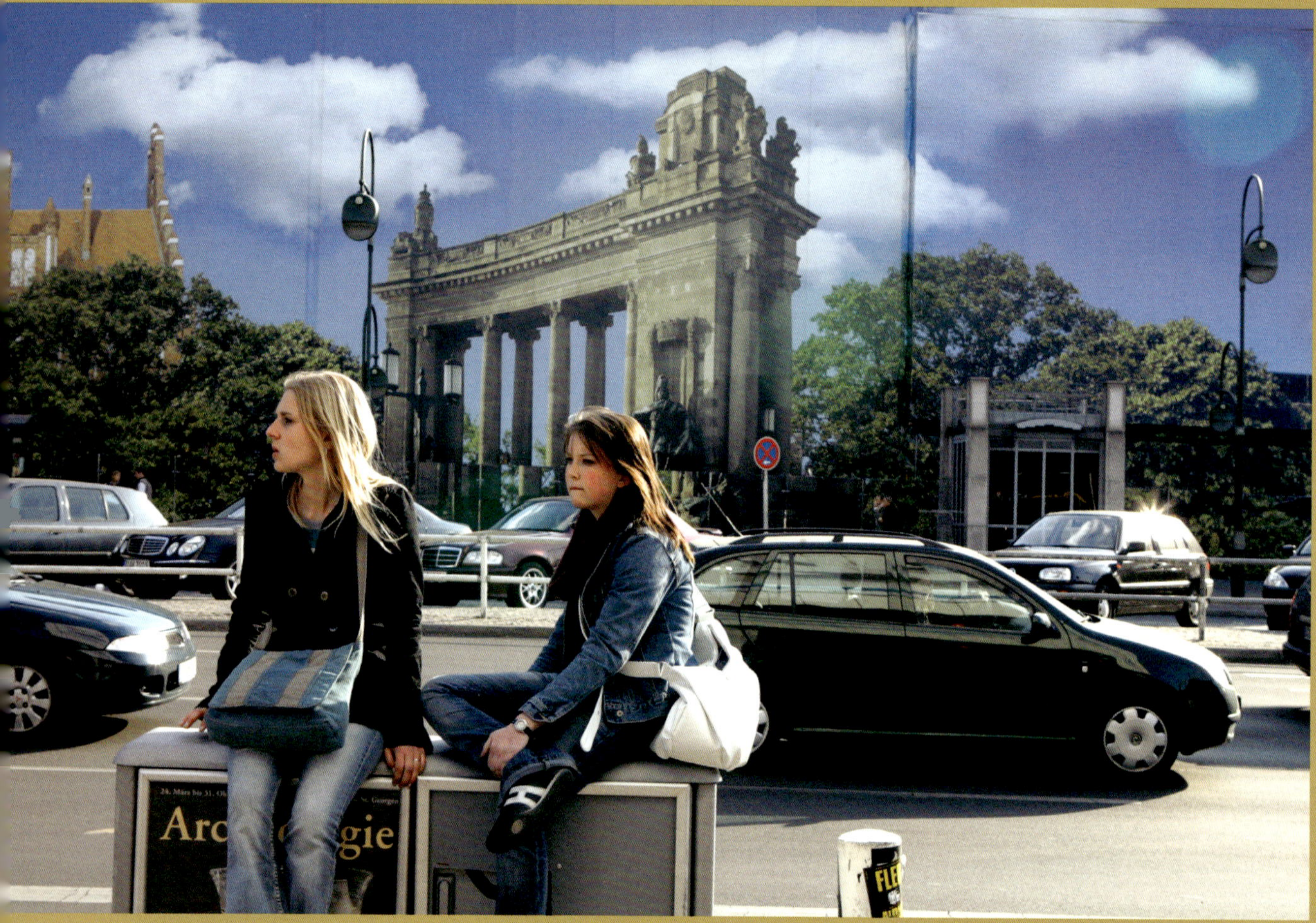

Bahnhof Zoo

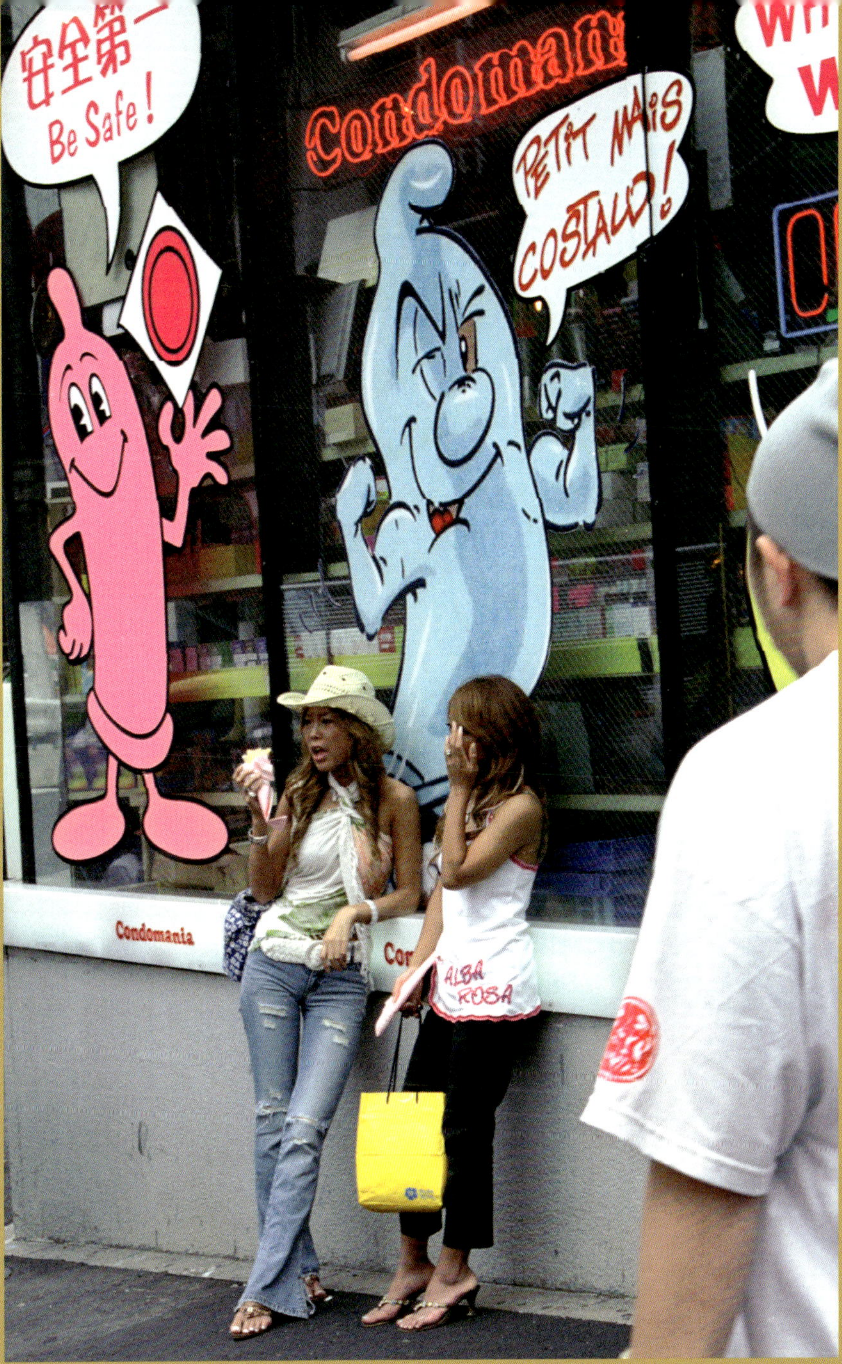
安全第一
Be Safe!
Condomania
PETIT MAIS COSTAUD!
Condomania
ALBA ROSA

Harajyuku

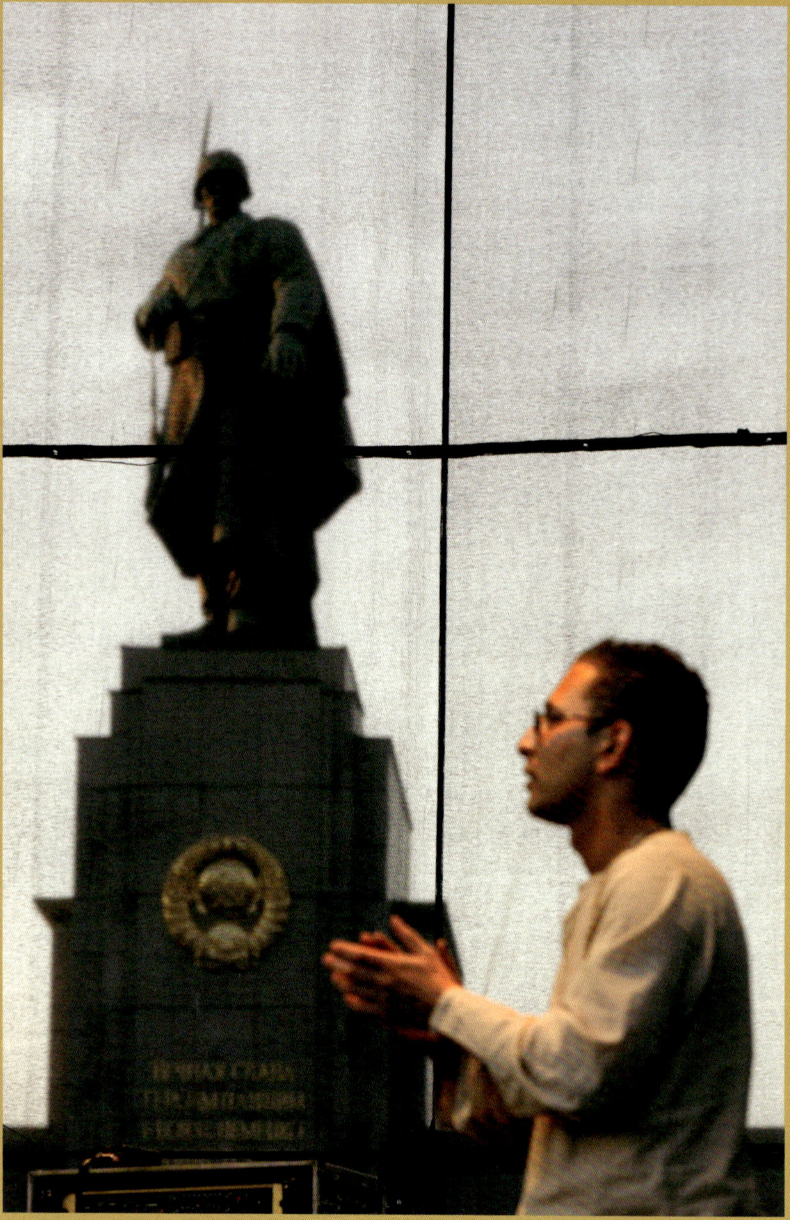

Straße des 17. Juni

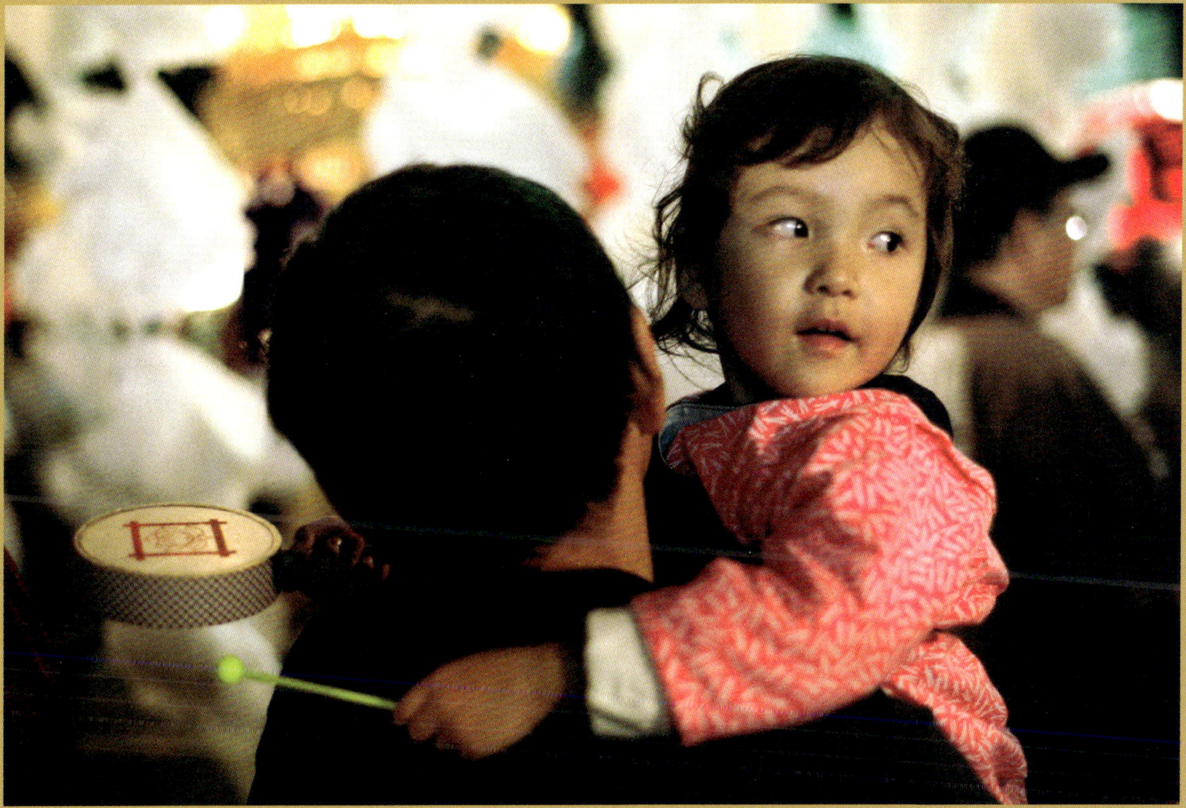

Ikegami

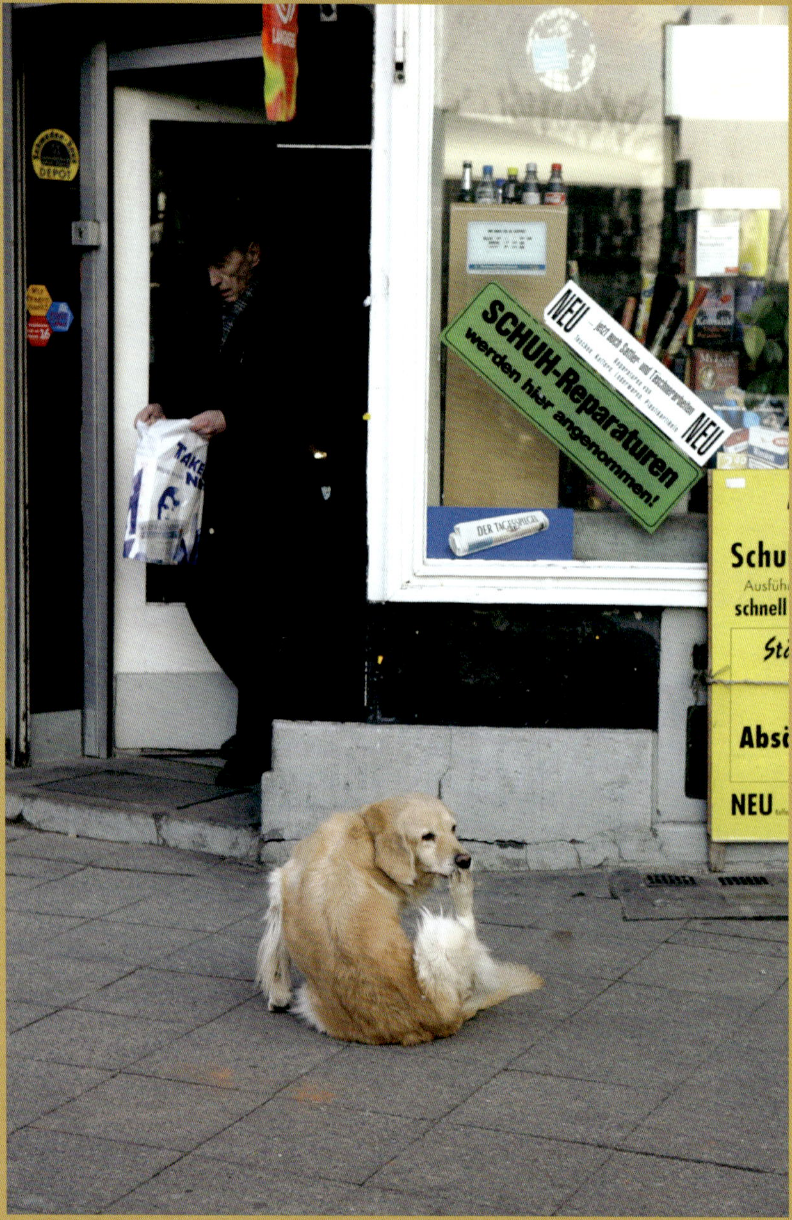

Wilmersdorf

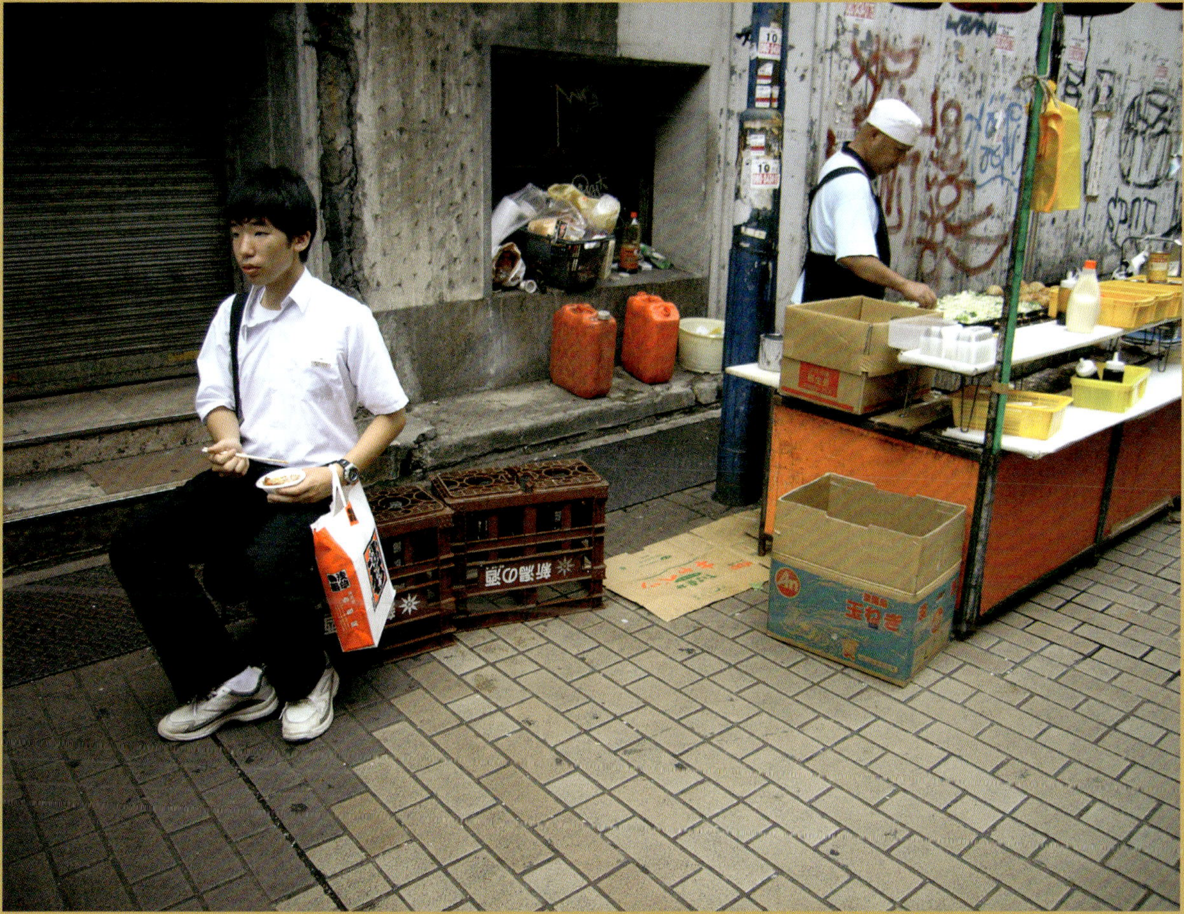

Ameyoko

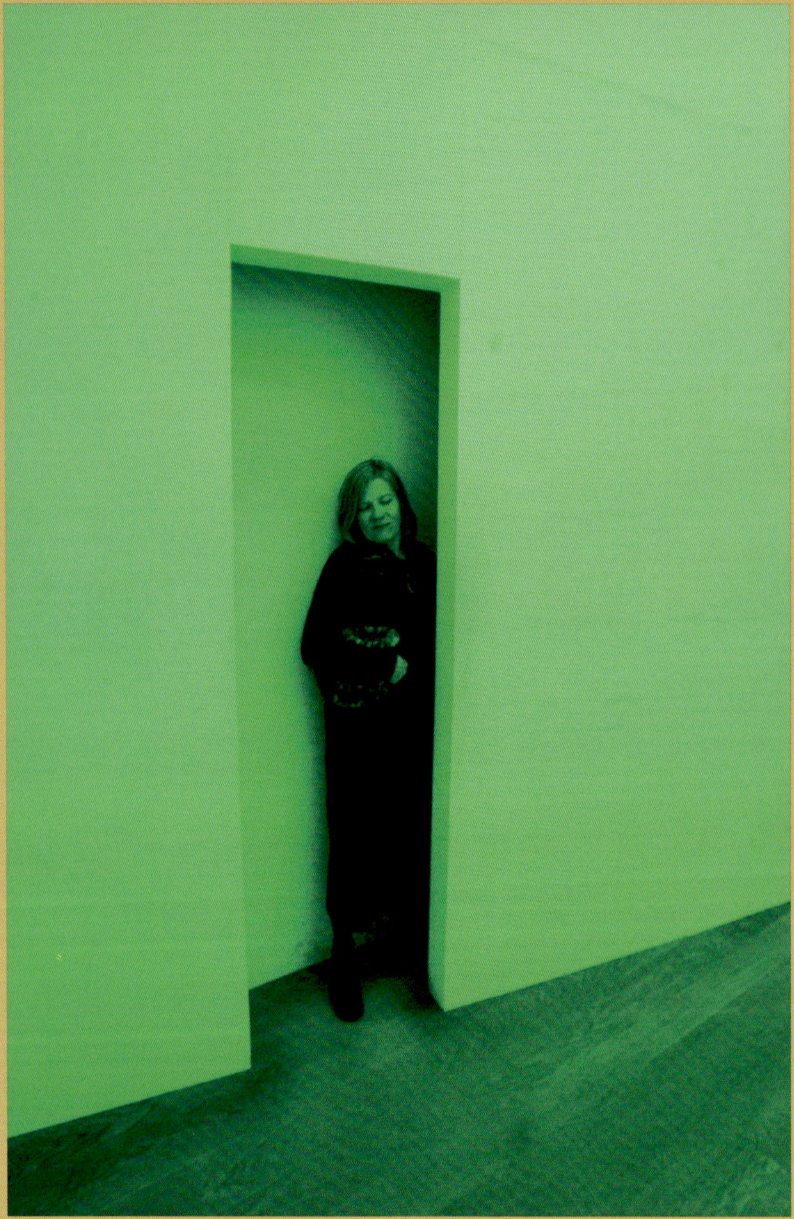

Hamburger Bahnhof – Museum für Gegenwart

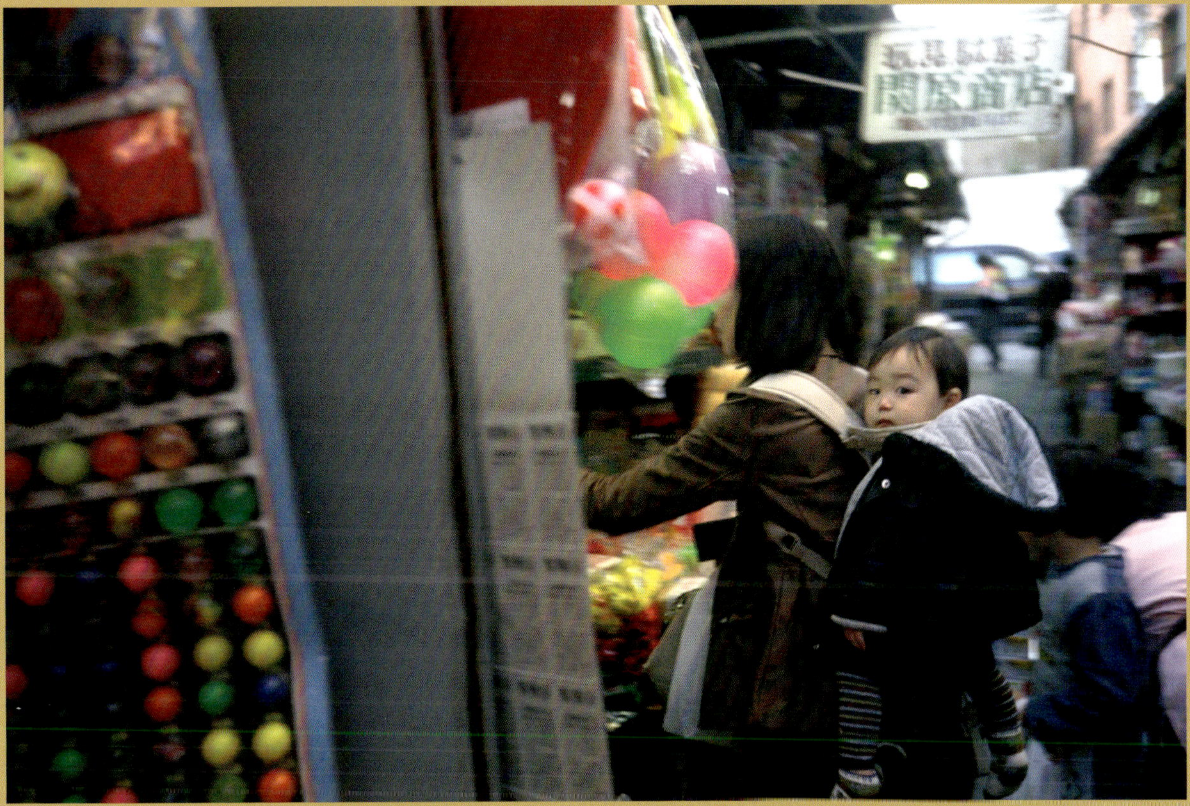

Nippori

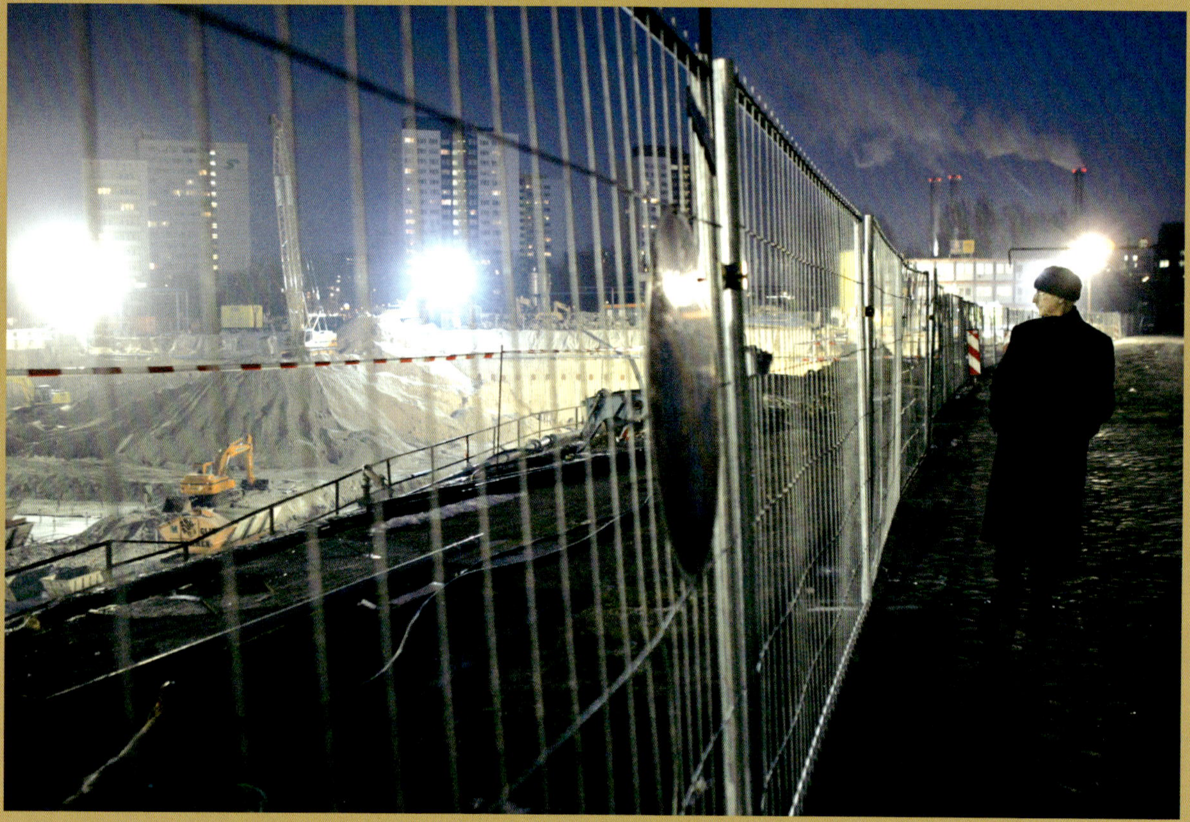

Rochstraße

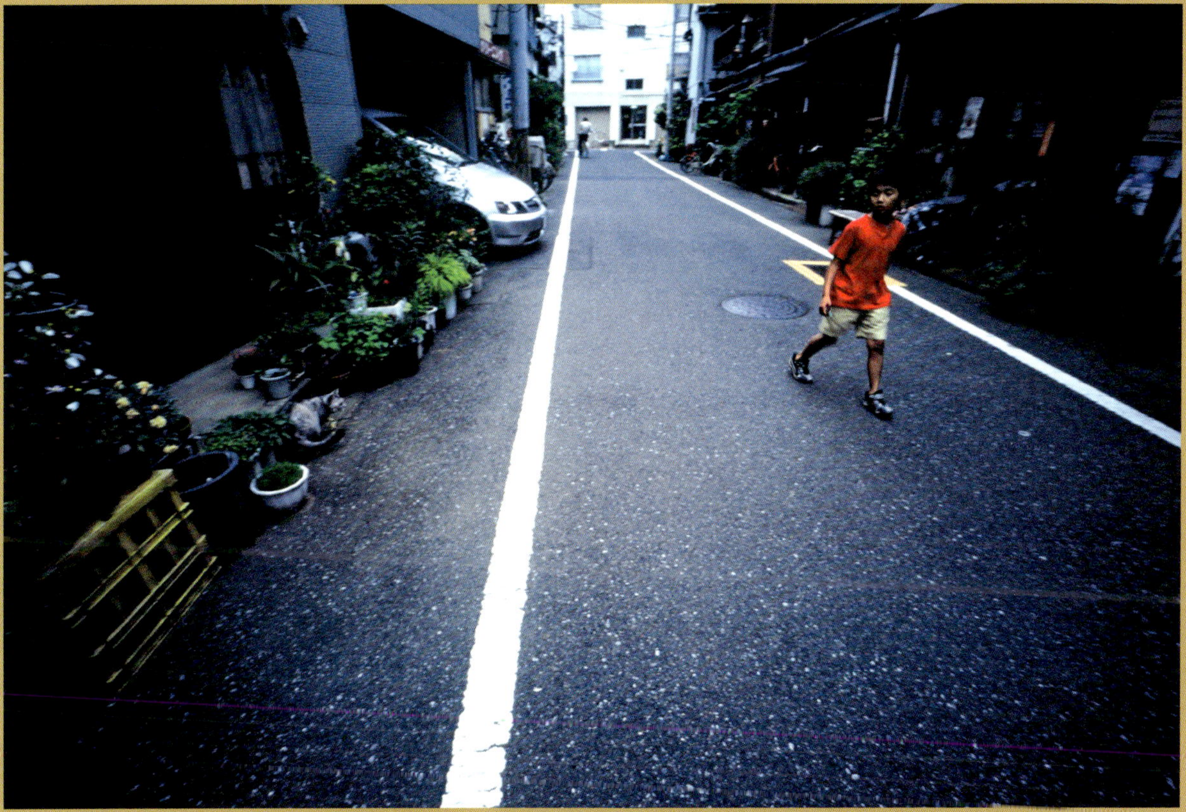

Shitaya

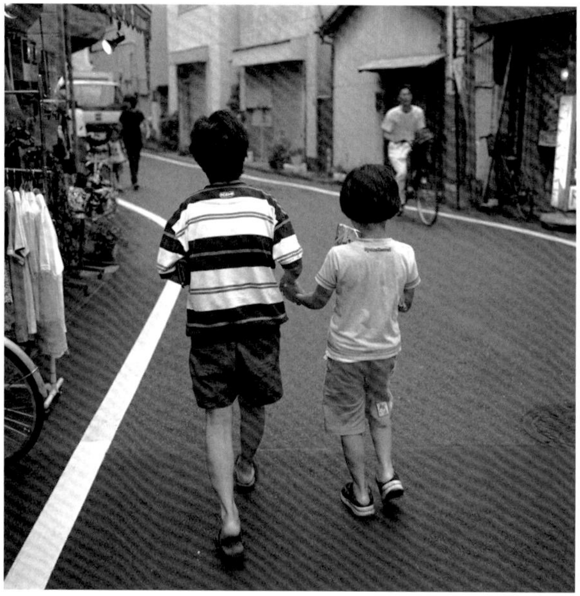

して、でき上がったベルリンの写真と東京の写真をトランプのようにシャッフルしてみた。案の定、それは違和感なく混在し、一つの世界を構成した。その中から、作品の見た目自体も似ているベルリンの写真と東京の写真を、見開きで並べたのが本写真集である。ただし、明らかにシチュエーションが同じものを並べてもつまらないので、なるべく「違うようでどこか似ている」あるいは「似ているがどこか違う」程度の微妙な関係性で選んだつもりである。「似ている」「似ていない」だけでなく、「ベルリン＋東京」の「＋」の部分から、どちらでもない新しい都市空間が生まれはしないか、という期待感を込めて。

二〇〇六年八月、東京の「下町」の自宅にて
内村 浩介

九

現在のベルリンと東京の共通点を挙げるとすれば、まず、第二次大戦後に廃墟から再生された街であるということだろう。ベルリン、特に西ベルリンの場合は、戦前の街区、建物のアウトラインを残しながら再生し、東京の場合は街区こそ基本的には変わっていないが、そこに乗っている建物はほとんどが全く新しいものに取って変わっているという点では異なる。だが、政治的な分断を経て尚も「工事中」であるベルリンと、戦後絶え間なく変化を続けている東京は、ほぼ完成されたプラハや京都などの古都にはない、動のエネルギーがある。東京では当たり前のように見られる古いものと新しいもののドラスティックな混在は、ヨーロッパにおいては珍しく、ベルリンでも目立っている。

第二に、複数の中心部を持つその都市形態である。ベルリンの場合は、クーダム周辺の旧西ベルリンの中心部と旧東ベルリンのアレキサンダー広場周辺、そして、その間にあるミッテ。東京にも、戦前の歓楽街の浅草・上野と、戦後に歓楽街として栄えた新宿・渋谷、そして戦前からの中心的商業地区である銀座がその中間にある。似たような役割を持ちながら、それぞれに個性があるのもよく似ている。ついでに言えば、他の大都市ではあまり見られない地上を走る鉄道（S-Bahn、JR線）がそれらの中心部を丸く囲っているのも同じだ。

かつて東西に分断されていた、という事実はベルリン固有のもので、今も東と西では街も人々の雰囲気も全く違うように見える。実は、これは東京にも当てはまる。東京は大きく東部の低地帯の「下町」と西部の台地に広がる「山の手」に分かれる。一般的には「下町」が古くからいる人たちが暮らす庶民の街、「山の手」が全国から集まってきた人たちが暮らす洗練された街とされている。最近は「下町」の古い街並が失われ、この区分は有名無実化しつつあるとも言われているが、私はそうは思わない。むしろよりはっきりしてきている。私は社会学者ではないので、日本の経済的、政治的変遷などを通じてその理由を語る資格はない。だが、長年東京で写真を撮っている一人として、そこで暮らす人々と街の雰囲気の違いは、はっきりと見てとれると断言できる。地味で落ち着いた「下町」と、きらびやかで忙しい「山の手」が、ちょうど旧東ベルリンと西ベルリンのようなコントラストを見せている。

勤勉でまじめと言われる両国の国民性など、一般的によく言われている共通点もまだあるが、これ以上挙げるのはもうやめておこう。実は、これまで自分なりにしてきた分析も、本写真集の写真を語るうえではあまり意味がないからだ。この写真集に収められた写真の中に、こうしたテーマを直接反映したものは一枚としてない。あくまでも、これらの事情を恐らくは背景にした共通した空気感を、個人の感性で切り取った写真に過ぎない。

ともかく、私は二〇〇五年の冬以降、東京でのライフワークの延長線上の作業として、同年の春と翌年の冬に立て続けにベルリンを訪れ、写真を撮った。そ

頃だろうか。多くのその年代の男の子同様、私も戦車とか戦闘機が大好きだった。中でもお気に入りはドイツもので（ドイツではある種のタブーになっている第二次大戦時のドイツ軍兵器は、日本ではプラモデルの主役である）、友人と競ってタイガー戦車などのプラモデルを作ったものである。そこから、ドイツの近代史や文化についても少しずつ興味を持つようになり、当時サッカーのワールドカップで活躍していたルムメニゲやリトバルスキーのプレーに憧れてサッカーも始めた。ロンドン時代はクラシック音楽に興味を持つようになり、特に（オーストリア人だが）モーツアルトに傾倒した。現代音楽も好きで、コヴェント・ガーデンで観たシュトックハウゼンの新作オペラは、その後の感性に大きな影響を与えるほど、ショッキングだった。帰国後、写真を始めてからはヴィム・ヴェンダーズの映像に傾倒した。そして、今はフォルクスワーゲンの車で出かけてカール・ツァイスのレンズで写真を撮っている。これらは意識して得られた嗜好ではなく、「いつのまにかそうなっていた」といった方が正しい。

ベルリンへのシンパシーの根っ子にあるのは、最初の訪問で受けた分断時代の強いイメージと、個人的な「ドイツ好き」な感性であるのは間違いない。しかし、一方で先に述べた「東京好き」な感性とリンクしているのも確かだ。なぜなら、二〇〇五年冬の二度目の訪問時に感じた、冒頭の「ベルリンと東京は似ている」という電撃的な直感が、本写真集刊行のきっかけになったからだ。

二度目の訪問のそもそもの目的は、ベルリンの近代建築を見ることだった。街頭スナップを撮っている者として建築には興味があったし、ちょうどその頃知り合った建築家の友人が、「統一後、再開発が進むベルリンの近代建築が今、面白い」と言っていたからだ。結局、その建築家と旧知のインテリアコーディネーターとベルリンを訪れたのだが、建築そのものから得たものもさることながら、建築巡りの合間に片手間に撮った街頭スナップが予想以上にしっくり来た。

それまでも、ロンドン、コペンハーゲン、カルカッタ（インド）、台北、香港、バンコク、成都（中国）など、外国で街頭スナップを撮ったことはあったが、それはライフワークの東京の写真とはリンクせず、その場限りのものだ。被写体から発せられるメッセージ、空気感が異質なものだったからだ。ところが、ベルリンでは、東京と全く同じ感覚で写真を撮れる。目の前に広がる風景は異質なのに、撮っている自分の気分は同じなのだ。東京のどこかで受けたことのあるメッセージを同じ感性で切り取った、と言い換えてもいい。

では、どのようなメッセージが同じかと問われると、実は明確に言葉で表現することはできない。言葉で表現できないから写真で表現しているのだ、とにかく写真を見てほしい、というのが本音だ。だが、それでは少々無責任なので、自分なりにその客観的な部分を分析してみよう。

意味で、私の写真にも「自分」が投影されているということは否定しない。だが、被写体が語りかけるメッセージそのものになるべくこだわりたい、という思いが強いのも事実だ。基本的には「自分の感性」と「被写体のメッセージ」のバランスの中で、私は後者にウェイトを置いて東京を撮ってきた。だから、東京に食い込みすぎず、むしろ傍観者に近い態度でカメラを構えている。

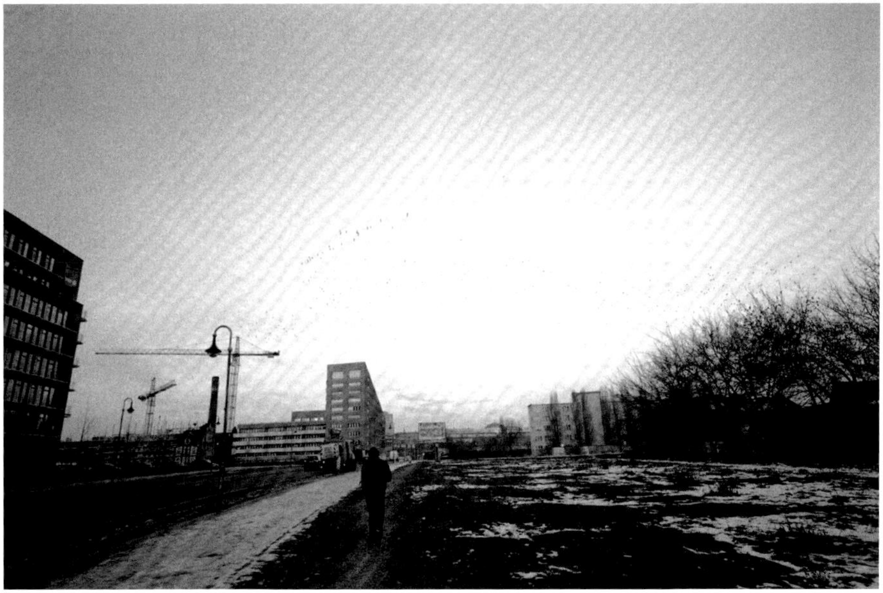

　一時期、それは写真家として不誠実ではないかと悩んだこともあったが、今はほとんど迷いはない。なぜなら、自分が東京を撮り続ける最大の理由が、その吐き出す空気感が単純に心地よく、それをカメラで切り取ることによって、最大限に感じたいからだと気づいたからだ。確かに、この街は騒音に包まれ、人々は虚栄に追われ、人口密度が気持ち悪いほどに高い。夏の気温と湿度は高すぎる。そういう大嫌いな個々の事象を差し置いても、この街の基礎となっている空気感、つまり人々や路上の物体、情景が訴えかけるメッセージはなぜだか心地良い。

　東京の心地よさの正体を語る前に、ベルリンとドイツの話をしたい。ベルリンを初めて訪れたのは、ロンドンに暮らしていた一九八四年。まだ壁で分断されていた冷戦の最前線を、外交官だった父の運転する車で東側から入った。まだ写真を始めていなかったし、家族旅行で観光地を回っただけなので、その時の印象をうまく言葉にはできないが、強烈なインパクトを受けたのは確かだ。「美しい」とか「荘厳」などという賛辞の言葉は当てはまらないが、ロンドンやパリとは明らかに違う空気感に不思議なシンパシーを感じた。それは東西に分断されているという異常な状況を含めて、街全体から発せられていたように思う。

　そもそも、私は「ドイツ的なもの」が子供の頃から好きだ。最初にそれに魅了されたのは、十二・三歳の

東京＋ベルリン

「ベルリンと東京は似ている」

この写真集の刊行を前にして、私は確信している。しかし、この言葉に共感する人はほとんどいないだろう。両都市に行った事があるのなら、なおさらだ。一般的な認識では、徹底した都市計画に基づいたヨーロッパの都市の「整然」と、自然発生的に成り立っているアジアの都市の「混沌」は対照的だし、一度建てた建築物を補修を繰り返しながら長く使う「石の文化」と、使い捨てに近い「木の文化」は根本的な発想が違う。ベルリンと東京というヨーロッパとアジアを代表する都市にもこれらは当てはまり、実際、都市空間として両者は異質である。

「ベルリンへ行くと、この都市の魅力は何なのだろうといつも思います。私自身は東京と共通なものを感じるというよりも、二都市を比較して、その違いの中にそれぞれの都市の文化の違いというものを感じるほうなのです」

これは、ドイツ全土を何度も訪れているある日本人のドイツ文化研究者の言葉だ。都市や文化への造詣が深い人ほど、ドイツ（ベルリン）と日本（東京）の「違い」を的確に把握し、両都市の個性を見いだす。そして、この見方は、専門家として、あるいは一旅行者として、正しいと思う。

一方、都市論や建築学の専門家ではない私は、写真家として長く東京という都市と向き合ってきた。具体的には、東京の街頭を行き交う人や路上にあるさまざまな不思議な物体、季節や街のざわめきが作り出す空気感をカメラという機械の目を通して切り取ってきた。東京に暮らす特定の人物や特定の街を追っているわけではない。いつもカメラを片手にフラリと街に出て、偶然出会った一期一会の情景を心のおもむくままに撮っている。

この一銭の収入にも名誉にも結びつかない行為を、なぜ自分は生活の一部のように繰り返してきたのだろう。写真を始めた十〇代の頃に出会った、アンリ・カルティエ・ブレッソンや木村伊兵衛の作品に感化されたからか？それも少しはある。ビルマで生まれ、少年時代の三分の二をカナダと英国で過ごしたことによる、日本人としてのアイデンティティーの希薄さを、東京を見つめることを通じて埋め合わせようとしたのだろうか？これはブレッソン云々よりも正解に近い。

だが、本当に自分のアイデンティティーと東京を重ね合わせたいのなら、もっと自分の肉体と精神を東京という街に食い込ませ、写真の中心に「自分」を据えていたはずだ。実際、周囲の同年代の写真家の多くは、より「自分が深く関わる街」または「自分を投影する風景」として、東京、あるいはその他の町のスナップを撮り、成功を収めている。

私の写真はその点で中途半端である。シ鉢ッターを押すのが感受性を持った人間である限り、望まなくとも押した「自分」は写真に写り込むものだ。その

下記の方々のご協力に感謝致します（敬称略）。

caco& ゴースケ & マメ
松村哲志 , 矢崎崇
生田千秋
柳田昭彦 , 西村佑子 , 溝井祐樹
浅井美砂
川原志津香
坂本亜由理

Colophone

翻訳（ドイツ語）: 川原志津香
翻訳（英語）: 大石美和
英語解説文編集 : Inez Templeton
ページデザイン・レイアウト : 浅井美砂
カバーデザイン : caco
印刷・製本 : OAN Offizin Andersen Nexö Leipzig, Zwenkau

Bibliographic information published by Die Deutsche Bibliothek
Die Deutsche Bibliothek lists this publication in the Deutsche Nationalbibliografie; detailed bibliographic data are available in the Internet at http://dnb.ddb.de

jovis Verlag
Kurfürstenstraße 15/16
10785 Berlin

www.jovis.de

ISBN: 978-3-939633-05-1

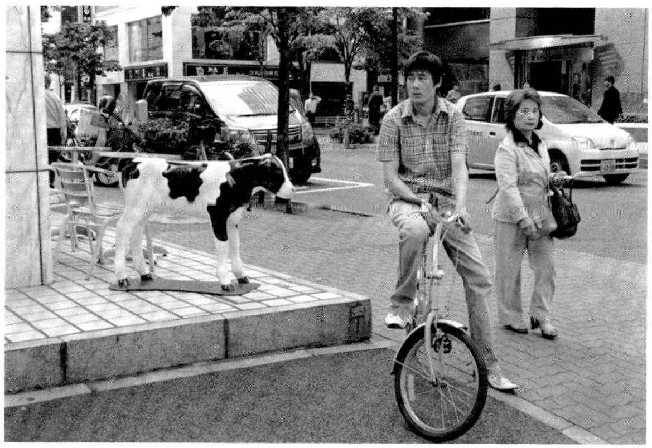

東京＋ベルリン

内村浩介

jovis

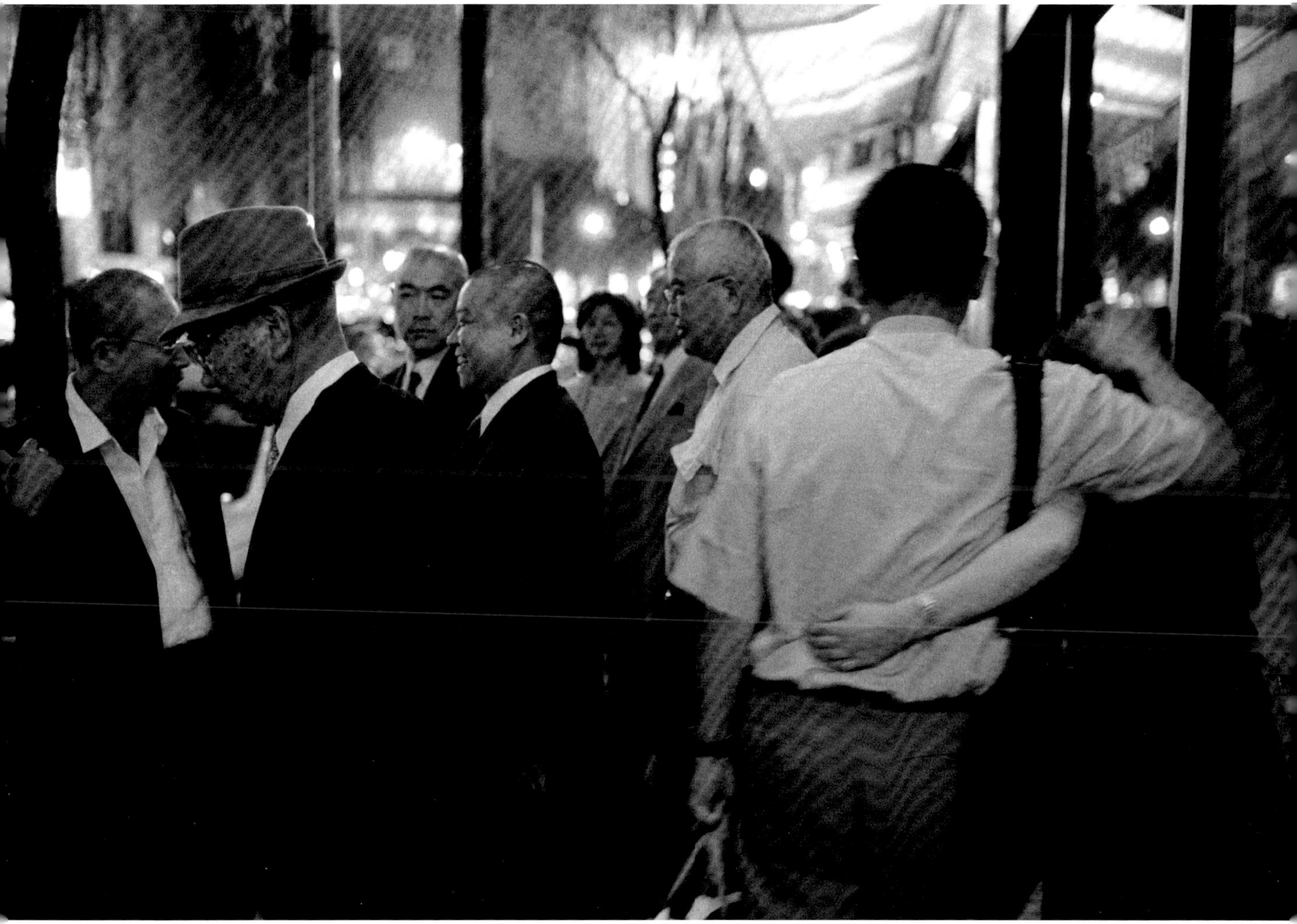

東京＋ベルリン

内村浩介

jovis